JESUS IN VERSES

A poetic portrayal of Jesus Christ

By

Deonaraine Ramdeo

"For God so loved the world that He gave His one and only Son, that whoever believes in Him shall not perish but have eternal life."

— John 3:16

Table of Contents

ACKNOWLEDGEMENT

First and foremost, I sincerely acknowledge and appreciate the inspiration and divine direction from God, the Creator of everything and everyone. I am grateful to the Almighty for using me as an instrument and medium to write and publish this book, dedicated to the life and works of the Lord and Saviour Jesus Christ. I am eternally thankful to God for giving me the intelligence, energy, patience, and wherewithal to complete "Jesus in Verses "as a gracious gift to the entire world.

I am grateful for the written and recorded material from the Holy Bible. In so doing, I acknowledge the efforts of the original authors of the books of the Bible, especially the Gospels in the New Testament, namely Matthew, Mark, Luke, and John. I am also grateful to Google for providing relevant information at the click of a button.

I owe a special vote of gratitude to the Christian neighbor who sparked my impulse to embark on the noble project of presenting Jesus Christ from a poetic perspective. Last but not least, I value and appreciate the support I received from my loving wife, who provided the encouragement I needed to stay on task until the end of the project.

I also acknowledge and appreciate the help and valuable advice provided by **USA Writers and Publishers.**

DEDICATION

I dedicate and present this book to the world at large, with the fervent hope that it will have a positive impact on people's lives. I am convinced that knowledge of, belief in, and adherence to Jesus and His teachings and blessings will illuminate, improve, and positively influence their lives.

I also dedicate this book to my family: my wife, Bibi, my son, Pooran, and his family. Special mention of note goes to my two sisters, Data and Vimla, and my two brothers, Ramesh and Jewel.

INTRODUCTION

I consider the writing of this book a divine duty and an ordained obligation to present Jesus and His ministry in a novel and noble perspective. Something quite different from the profusion of prose presentations. Writing **"Jesus in Verses"**

I deliberately chose to adopt a poetic approach, departing from ordinary prose.

Prose is pointed, powerful, and parched, but poetry is alive and artful. Prose appeals to the brain, the rational, whereas poetry appeals to the heart, the emotional.

I chose to present Jesus in poetry, which is more exciting and exotic, as it opens a fresh appeal to readers. I was motivated by a neighbor, a woman who is a faithful follower of Jesus Christ. She had read my first book, entitled "Silent, Silvery Stream." and was impressed by its format and presentation. So much so that she encouraged me to write about Jesus similarly. This noble nudge to write about Jesus brightened a bulb in my brain. Like a blessed bang from the blues, it hit my conscience with indescribable inspiration to enter divine territory to tell Jesus' story.

Spiritually, cautiously, I embarked on the pleasant task of compiling verses covering the life and works of Jesus. I felt that this was a way for me to express my deep gratitude to God and His Universe for the blessings upon my family and me. So, with alacrity and enthusiasm,

I started to write. Based on my personal knowledge and background in Christianity, I put down on paper one page at a time. I had done Scripture as a London-based examinable subject at the GCE level. I also benefited from lectures, lessons, and literature from a Canadian priest on a mission to Guyana. With his support and exposure to church services, sermons, and religious rituals, I gained substantial knowledge in Christianity. I also enjoyed reading the books of the Bible. Most of what I presented came from the four Gospels in the New Testament.

My years of service as an ordained Catechist in one of the churches in the Bahamas

Parish forced me to dig deep into ecclesiastical and Biblical matters. This consolidated my knowledge of Christianity and opened the window to wend my way into writing this book.

By no means did I cover or touch on everything about Jesus' ministry. I deliberately stuck to the prominent and pertinent parts which encompass a decent portrayal of the prince of Peace, Lord of Lords and King of Kings.

The book started with the prediction of Jesus' coming to earth as the righteous Representative of God. The Bible is replete with passages that foretold the advent and mission of God's chosen One. Prophets and angels foretold the coming of the Messiah and Saviour.

His humble birth in a stable represents the most popular and beloved story of Advent and Nativity. This component of Christianity appeals tremendously to His followers and believers. It marks the most festive and glamorous high point celebrated worldwide, with Mass, carols, the exchange of gifts, decorations, and fancy lights, that herald goodwill and peace on earth.

Joseph, Jesus' earthly father, knew that his wife, Mary, was conceived by the Holy Ghost, so he was understanding and showed acceptance, patience, and care for Mary, the mother of God. In obedience to fulfill the tax requisition by the government, he had to go to Galilee to be registered in the region of his birth. There in Galille they could not get a room in the inn, so they settled in the stable where Jesus was born. Baby Jesus was visited by shepherds and wise men who glorified and worshipped Him. When King Herod learned that Jesus was coming to challenge him for the throne, he became jealous and furious. He asked the wise men to take him to Jesus so he could worship Him. Informed by angels, the wise men tricked Herod and did not return to him. Realizing that he had been tricked, he ordered that all newborn sons up to two years old be killed.

Guided by angels, Joseph took Mary and son to safety. Divine intervention occurred many times to safeguard Jesus. As a child, Jesus was nurtured and raised like any other child of the time. Blessed Mary ensured that Jesus was raised in a righteous, God-fearing manner. As a youngster, Jesus faithfully followed His parents to Sunday service and special holidays. On occasion, Jesus remained behind after church to discuss and debate spiritual matters with priests and elders. They were surprised by His wealth of knowledge at such a young age. Besides spiritual pursuits, Jesus learned to be a carpenter under Joseph's tutorship, becoming an established carpenter.

When Jesus became an adult, he quickly established His independence and went about on His own accord, guided by divine guidance. He knew the importance of baptism, so He went to the River Jordan to be baptized by John the Baptist. It was a historic lesson in humility when a higher power stooped down to be baptized by a lesser power. Even God saluted this encounter via heavenly utterance and celebratory acts of acknowledgement.

Mention is made of His temptation by Satan in the wilderness for forty days and forty nights, which He victoriously overcame by pertinent reference to Scripture. Even the mighty Devil gave up in defeat against the power and authority of God.

Jesus then chose twelve disciples to accompany Him during His ministry. Together, they traversed long and far territories to teach and preach the word of God. With no motorized means of transportation, they set out on foot to undertake the noble task of spreading the good news. As people recognized and appreciated His great influence and power, they voluntarily helped in whatever way they could. They offered them food, shelter, and convenience. The boats and ships used to sail across lakes and seas were provided by capable volunteers.

In the fashion of a hunter-gatherer manner, they feasted on fresh fruits and vegetables and fish. Benefiting bountifully from the divine powers of Jesus, fishermen caught fish in abundance in overfished and unproductive waters. Fish played an important part in Jesus' life and works. So much so, they prided themselves as fishers of men.

Always thronged by multitudes, Jesus employed parables and miracles to enhance His teachings. He demonstrated unconditional love and support to children, people with low incomes, and people in need. He instantly healed the sick and raised the dead, thus boosting His popularity and authority.

All good things come to an end. Jesus made His triumphant entry into Jerusalem, where He was welcomed and hailed as the righteous revolutionary who would satisfy the crowds' demands for justice and relief from the current government's oppression. They failed to realize that Jesus came to win hearts and souls through peaceful, loving measures, not to compete with or challenge the emperor. Deeply disappointed, the multitude, supported by the Jewish elders and priests, went on a rampage to eliminate Him. They fomented and fabricated baseless contention that Jesus posed a mortal and existential threat to civil society. They accused Him of treason, destruction of the temple, blasphemy, and His desire to be King of the Jews.

At the evil orchestration of a religious trial, he was deemed guilty of blasphemy and was condemned to death. Since the Chief Priest did not have the authority to execute criminals, Jesus was hurriedly hauled to a civil trial under Pontius Pilate, the presiding governor vested with the power to order the execution of convicted criminals. Despite the preponderance of falsified testimonies, the Governor could not find Jesus guilty of any crimes. Herod's intervention did not help much. To prevent a civil upheaval or revolt, Pilate reluctantly gave in to the crowd's demands to crucify Jesus instead of Barabbas.

Bravely, confidently, Jesus faced His trials and tortures and submitted to crucifixion. Public opinion questioned Jesus' refusal to save Himself as He had saved others. Critics of Christianity to date want to know why the all-powerful Christ failed to save Himself. Jesus knew what was predicted and ordained, so He submitted to fulfill the Scripture. He knew long before his impending ultimate sacrifice that His death and resurrection would become the foundation on which Christianity would flourish.

The book also touches on the aftermath of His death and His subsequent reunion with His disciples as the risen Lord, a testimony to His eternal divine power and His ascension to sit at the right hand of God. He died to save us. His blood washes us.

PRECIOUS PROPHESIES

Prophecy, the predictive practice in nature
The art and ability to foretell the future
A godly gift given to selected agents
Channels announcing profound future events

Forecasts focus on tomorrow's happenings.
Affording people a precautionary warning
Prophecy predicts proceedings over a long time
Which people expect to happen down the line

The prophecy of the birth of Jesus
It was preliminary, profuse, but precious
Noted and quoted in numerous contexts
Which generations received with prestige and pretexts

The Old and New Testaments record prophecy
Of a promised Messiah to humanity
An eminent and everlasting Saviour
A Prince of Peace and a Wonderful Counselor

2 Samuel 7: A promise was presaged
That is a descendant of David's lineage
Would establish an everlasting Kingdom in reality
Which eventually turned out to be Christianity

In Micah 5:2, the Magi beat the prophetic drum
O Bethlem Ephrathah, from you shall come
A Ruler of Israel, an anointed Pearl
The King of Kings of the entire world

Isaiah 7:14 proclaimed the Immaculate Conception.
When the Lord Himself shall make direct intervention
Beholding a virgin to bear a son for all
And shall call His name Immanuel

Isaiah 9:6-7 declared that a child is born to us
A sacred sign given, princely and precious
His name shall be called Wonderful Counselor
But the gov't shall be on his shoulder

Malachi 3:1 foretells the coming of the Lord to the temple
A Messenger of the Covenant will come plain and simple
Subsequent events revealed Christ visiting the temple
Following God's pronounced principle

Jeremiah 23: 5-6 prophesies the birth of Jesus
As a Branch from David's line, so righteous
Who will bring salvation and holiness
And shall it be called "The Lord of the Righteous."

Luke 1:67-79 outlines Zechariah's song of prophecy
Echoing the coming of a great Personality
The "Horn of Salvation "is super and solid
A descendant of the house of David

Luke 1;26-38 specifically captures the precious prophecy
Where angel Gabriel delivers the good news to Mary
A virgin betrothed to Joseph
Soon to get married in Nazareth

Hail Mary, thou art highly favored
The Lord is with Thee, blessed and covered
Troubled by this sudden salutation
But She was assured by the angel's favorable persuasion

And behold, thou shalt conceive in thy womb
A Son, whom thou shalt bring forth soon
And you shall call his name Jesus
Who shall be known as the Son of the Highest

Skeptical Mary questioned the possibility
Of her having a baby while still in virginity
The Holy Ghost shall come upon the
And a holy miracle will bless thee with a baby

Behold the handmaid of the Lord.
Be it unto me according to thy word
And upon Mary's blessed assurance
Angel Gabriel departed from her presence

The name Jesus came from the Hebrew Yeshua.
Translated to carry the meaning Saviour
Evolved from Hebrew to Greek as Jesous
And finally, in Latin and English as Jesus

The name Jesus was given by angelic instruction
Which means "the Anointed One. "
With the divine purpose of bringing salvation
And to deliver people from spiritual bondage and oppression

Biblical injunctions tell us how
At the name of Jesus, every knee shall bow
Mary's duty was to deliver Jesus
To the world and all of us

Then Mary visited her cousin Elizabeth in Judea
Mary's salutation created a great wonder
Elizabeth was filled with the Holy Ghost
Knowing that the mother of her Lord is a blessed boast

Being espoused to Mary, Joseph wondered.
Over the pregnancy, he had not empowered
Persuaded in a dream by the Lord's angel
Joseph accepted Mary as his wife in good standing

John, the voice in the wilderness
Preached about a mightier One, an unknown Jesus
Whose shoes' latchet he was unworthy to untie
But ordained to baptize Him as the Most High

There are countless pertinent prophecies to suffice
The appearance of Lord and Savior Jesus Christ
Validating God's wish and wisdom
Giving a blessed beacon to burn bright in Christendom

THE MAGNIFICAT: Mary's Song of Praise

My soul magnifies the Lord.

And my spirit rejoices in God my Savior

For He has looked on the humble estate of His servant

For behold, from now on all generations will call me blessed

For He who is mighty has done great things for me

And holy is His name

And His mercy is for those who fear Him from generation to generations

He has shown strength with His arm

He has scattered the proud in the thoughts of their hearts

He has brought down the mighty from their thrones

And exalted those of humble estate

He has filled the hungry with good things

And the rich He has sent away empty

He has helped His servant Israel

In remembrance of His mercy

As He spoke to our fathers

To Abraham and to His offspring forever.

Mary expressed her gratitude to God in a song

Happy to be the Mother of a newborn

Specially selected as a virgin in innocence

Blessed with the immaculate task of deliverance

Of Jesus into the world, anointed and incarnated

To forgive sins of the living and the departed

The song of praise sung by Mother Mary

Glorified and underscored a divine duty

A pious phenomenon, she gladly accepted

With heart and soul completely contented
The consummate expression of joy
Reverberated sweet sentiments she did employ
Normally, when people are joyful, they sing
To bring out the deep feelings within
Chanting the lovely lyrics loudly
Signalling to the world very clearly
That they are up on cloud nine
So sweet, so sublime
Mary's profound praise in a hymn
Celebrated God's love, unique and unending
Her soul magnified God's mercy and justice
Elevating the humble, and humbling the mighty and the rich
A prophetic rendition of God's faithfulness
Filling the hungry with things abundantly blessed
Mary's poem of praise to the Lord
Teaches us to be of one accord
Under God's grace and guidance
Following lessons from divine deliverance
The Magnificat touches the soul, making it uncomfortable
To realize that sins signify trouble
It's a catalytic canticle to surrender
To a restructured social order
That reflects God's love, mercy, and laws
Allowing us to live lasting lives without flaws
The new social order regulates the haughty and rich
And includes the poor in the profitable pitch
It must heighten the heart of humility

Alter the arrogance of the high and mighty
Even the playing field for all
The essence of the Magnificat's call.

BIRTH OF JESUS

To raise needed money
Caesar Augustus sent out a decree
All must go to their original city
To be taxed accordingly

Joseph took Mary to Galilee
Unto Bethlehem, David's city
Because he was of David's lineage
A birthright of humble homage

Galilee to Bethlehem, a journey in jeopardy
Joseph trudged along as Mary rode on a donkey
One late evening, they stopped at an inn
Unfortunately, they had no room to sleep in

The only accommodation available
Was the low, humble stable
They hitched hay to make a bed
Where they lay their weary heads

There, Mary brought forth her memorable Son
Wrapping Him in swaddling clothes was no fun
Baby Jesus peacefully lay in a manger
The lowly, blessed beginning of our Saviour

There in the same country.
Shepherds were in the fields, busy
Keeping watch over their flocks
When an angel visited in silent shock

The shepherds were afraid to go to the helm
As the glory of the Lord shone around them
Fear not: I bring good tidings of great joy
For you, born on this day, a Saviour boy

Suddenly, a multitude of heavenly hosts
Joined the angel, chanting praises to the Holy Ghost
Glory to God in the highest Heaven
For peace on earth and goodwill toward men

The shepherds walked all the way to Bethlehem
To witness the gracious gift from Heaven
Finding Mary and Joseph with the babe in the manger
They rejoiced, gave praise, and spread the news all over

Wise men came from the east with grace
Guided by a star to Jesus' birthplace.
Coming to see the newborn King of the Jews
Following the written prophetic news

After following the star for many days
They finally found the place where Jesus lay
They fell and worshipped Him and Her
And presented gifts of gold, frankincense, and myrrh

The wise men had told King Herod of a new King
Who would become the new ruler, challenging him
Hiding his envy, he asked them to bring the new King
So, he, Herod, could glorify and worship Him

Troubled by such news, Herod ordered his men
To kill all boys under two years old, then
Later, the wise men were warned by God
So, they never returned with news to Herod

When the wise men and shepherds departed
An angel in Joseph's dream visited
Warning him to leave Judaea in secret
And take Jesus and Mary across to Egypt

Upon the death of Herod and his deadly decree
The Lord appeared in Joseph's dream, telling him to flee
From Egypt, and go into the land of Israel
Joseph obeyed, taking Mary and the child

Jesus was taken to the church to be blessed thereon
By a devout priest named Simeon
Who the Holy Ghost promised he would not die
Until he had seen the Saviour, Most High

Simeon took baby Jesus in his arms
Praised God and blessed Jesus, the Holy Charm
Saying "Mine eyes have seen Thy salvation
Let me, thy servant, depart in peaceful cessation

Solemn Simeon, inspired by the Holy Ghost
Said to Mary in words of prophetic boast
"This child is set for fall and rise in Israel."
A precursor of death and the rising of the Anointed Pearl

At that moment, the prophetess Anna
Gave thanks to God for such a Saviour
As a faithful servant of God, she prophesied
That the Son of Salvation had arrived

Upon the accomplishment of eight days
Jesus was circumcised following the purification rites
And He was presented to the Lord in the temple
Was blessed as the Light to lighten all people

All things are performed according to the laws of the Lord.
They returned to Galilee in one accord
Where the child grew strong in spirit and body
Filled with the wisdom and grace of great Glory

Complying with customary patterns and traditions
Sons followed fathers in fashion and occupation
And so, Jesus became a carpenter
Working along with Joseph, his earthly father

Growing up in the home circle of Galilee
Jesus gained wisdom about the world and spirituality
Under the gracious guidance of Mother Mary
And stewardship of Joseph, His career company

When Jesus was a twelve-year-old youngster
He accompanied His parents to the Jerusalem Passover
Following the crowd of kinsfolk and acquaintances
They participated in the religious observance

Returning home in the spirit of merriment
Mary and Joseph realized that Jesus was absent
They returned looking for the missing Son
And finally found Him in the long run

After three days, they found Him in the temple
Sitting with priests and educated people
Discussing and debating critical religious matters
The panel was surprised at Jesus' questions and answers

Mary approached and asked Jesus.
"Why didn't you return with us?
Your father and I, in sorrow, search for Thou
And after anxious days, we found you now

Jesus replied, "How is it ye sought me?
I am here in good company.
In all earnest and in ease
Doing my father's business

JESUS BAPTISM

Baptism represents dying to life in sin
And rising to a newness to walk in
Basically, it is an act of Absolution
And an initiatory rite of Purification

Baptism is an act of obedience.
And a public declaration of religious allegiance
It is a ceremonial covenant of cleansing
And a qualification for active participation is believing

In baptism, water is a significant entity
A blessed ceremonial instrumentality
To cleanse and wash away sins
And create a new beginning

Baptismal water is used in three dimensions
Sprinkling on the head in the act of Aspersion
Pouring over the head in the act of Affusion
Or submersion of the body in the act of Immersion

During the amazing John and Jesus encounter
Baptism was done in running water
John baptized people in the River Jordon
Here, he baptized Jesus under the heavenly cordon

John chided Jesus in the baptismal plea
"You should be baptizing me."
Jesus received John's baptism in earnest.
In fulfillment of all righteousness

Upon Jesus baptism in the River Jordon
The Heavens opened in blessed abandon
And the Spirit of God descended like a dove
With a loud, laudable approving voice from above

The Heavenly voice declared from above.
This is my son, whom I dearly love
With Him, I am very pleased
Everyone was delighted with brilliant ease

Jesus' baptism fulfilled the Scriptural requirement.
The rite of righteousness and obedient fulfillment
An anointment and a divine affirmation
Of peace, purity, sanctity, and commemoration

Jesus, being sinless, needed no baptism.
He could have displayed divine dynamism.
But he chose to share the human experience
Becoming the Lamb of God is of great significance

His example provided a pattern of behavior
Who choose to become His followers
Demonstrating perfect obedience to God
A commitment and dedication to the Lord

Baptism is a fundamental practice of Christianity
A vital step into the blessed Holy Trinity
Symbolizing a death to sin
A consecrated covenant of a fresh beginning

At baptism, sanctified and consecrated water
Is applied thrice on the new believer
Being initiated in the name of the Father, Son, and Holy Ghost
A ceremonial absolution and purgatory toast

Performance of baptismal rites in the course of history
Varied according to denominations and dynasty
Some practiced sprinkling or pouring holy water
Others preferred triple immersion in the flowing river

THE TEMPTATIONS

Temptation is the act of alluring.
A seductive trap in the making
Temptation is not submission to wrong
It is the opening of the door to transgression

Temptations test one's mind and body.
Offering attractions in sweet shades of subtlety
To see if one can abstain or bend over
Revealing the strength of character

Failure on the tests of temptation
Shows weakness, sinfulness, and damnation
Passing the tests of temptation
Demonstrate discipline and determination

Falling into temptation is human and fine
Not succumbing to temptation is divine
History provided one excellent example
Of triumph over the temptation of the Devil

Immediately after his baptismal blessedness
The Spirit led Jesus into the wilderness
For forty days and forty nights duration
Fearlessly facing the tests of Satan's temptation

The Holy Spirit chose the wilderness.
To test Jesus' strength and weakness
If he failed and succumbed to temptation
His Holiness would be called into question

Being focused on food deprivation
The Devil came up with the first temptation
If you are the Son of the Godhead
Command this stone to become bread

Jesus answered in a confident tone.
Man shall not live by bread alone
But by every word of God
Who is our provident Lord

Taking Jesus to a high mountain
Satan showed him the Kingdoms that the earth did sustain
All of that I will gladly give to the
If you bow down and worship me

Jesus said, "Get behind me, Satan."
For it is written and sent from heaven
Thou shalt worship the Lord thy God
And only Him shall thou serve with laud

On the third temptation on the temple top
He asked Jesus to do a downward hop
And let the God in You
Bring angels to the miraculous rescue

Jesus responded, "Thou shalt not tempt the Lord thy God."
Indicating that to do so was bad
Frustrated by his failure in his effort
Satan departed in despair and hurt

Jesus resisted each of the three temptations
By presenting pertinent scriptural invocation
Aided by angelic and the ministering Spirit
And was finally delivered as the triumphant Prophet

Each temptation was a test of faith
A spiritual challenge at the gate
A verdict on virtue and a trial of willpower
To resist Satanic schemes to destroy and devour

Jesus' temptation symbolizes human struggle and suffering
The daily battle with life and living
Which must be overcome by personal preference
To succumb or to resist by scriptural reference

At the termination of the temptation over Thee
Jesus returned in the power of the Spirit to Galilee
His righteous fame spread throughout the region
A testimony of his victory over Satan

A common thread in temptation is the lust of the flesh
Turning stone into bread for hunger redress
The struggle with physical desire
Must be opposed by quoting scripture

The desires and lust of the flesh
Challenge the willpower in duress
To choose physical, personal gratification
Or to wait on God's plan and provision

Another trend in temptation is pride of position
Wielding the power of a worldly kingdom
The allure of station and status
Can be surmounted by the example of Jesus

Another thorn in temptation resides in the envy of eyes
Pursuing and piling up possessions to the skies
Pray for the possession of the Holy Spirit
By following Jesus' pattern to the limit

Temptations can be thwarted at your command
If you use the Bible as the sword in your hand
Jesus counteracted each temptation by saying, "It is written."
Read and quote what's appropriate and proven.

Beware of the deceptive temptation.
To quote scripture in the wrong situation
People quote scripture for personal gain
Which God nor truth shall sustain

Resistance to temptation demonstrates personal power.
Based on spiritual guidance and the strength of character
A willingness to live by God's plan
And not the dictates and designs of Satan

Fasting strengthens the ability to reject temptation
Not for forty days, but a 40-hour duration
Abstinence weakens urges and desires
As attention is focused on scripture

Victory over temptation shows stamina and sacredness
His baptism emphasizes cleanliness and righteousness
Tall testimonies to His Godliness
In a Kingdom that has no end or rest

THE BEATITUDE

Jesus delivered the blessed Beatitude.
To a great assembled multitude
Saying the poor in spirit
Will receive heavenly benefits
Mourners will obtain comfort
The meek will inherit the earth
The merciful will attain mercy
The pure in heart God they shall see
Peacemakers will become children of God
The wrongfully persecuted are going to the house of the Lord
Those reviled for Jesus' sake
Will have an exceeding reward to take
Let your light shine through your good deeds
And be glorified with great speed
Love your enemies and do good to them
Give alms, give and spend
Don't judge or condemn the living
Forgive you so that you will be forgiven
First, cast the beam from your eye
Before pulling out mote in thy brothers' eyes
Treasures come from good hearts
Evil hearts produce rotten fruits of all sorts
Build on a solid foundation
To avoid decline and destruction

MIRACLES OF JESUS

Miracles are extraordinary events or happenings.
Without natural or scientific groundings
Cannot be explained by any logical definition
Inconceivable by any stretch of the imagination

Miracles are attributed to a supernatural mystery'
Powered by invisible, imperceptible energy
Seen as signs of divine dynamics
Or the timely intervention of Godly theatrics

Miracles evoke and inspire awe and wonder
In those who are witnessing the divine drama
Leaving them speechless and shocked
Beyond belief, trying to take stock

Jesus performed several miracles during His ministry
Thus, proving His spiritual mission and divine ability
And demonstrating God's power through Him
To do works of wonder through thick and thin

Jesus' miracles demonstrated influential acts over Nature
Extensive healing, exorcism, and providing succor
Resurrection and reversion to perfection
All revealing supernatural power and compassion

Jesus first and famous miracle on the line
Was to turn water into wine
At a wedding feast in Cana in Galilee
A divine drama done dutifully

Mary and Jesus were guests.
Attending a wedding meek and modest
Celebration went to a woeful brink
As they ran out of wine to drink

Mindful Mary made the observation
And asked Jesus to help in such a situation
Jesus ordered that six pots be filled with water
And the miraculous transformation he did deliver

When the ruler of the feast tasted the wine
He acknowledged that the wine was fine
And asked why they kept the good wine for the last
As everyone enjoyed the blessed blast

The water in a pool in Jerusalem
Was noted to heal the sick and forsaken
A sick man, helpless, lay on the ground nearby
Waiting for his turn, his sickness to defy

When Jesus came by and passed by the pavement
He noticed the sick man's predicament
He said, "Rise, take up thy bed and walk."
Immediately, the man rose to his feet and talked.

Discovering that Jesus healed on the Sabbath
The Jews were furious that Jesus did that
Jesus told them that God had nothing against that
To save a life or to heal on the Sabbath

Faced with the task of feeding a multitude
Jesus and his disciples couldn't afford to buy food
With the bit of money they had at their disposal
They wondered how they could feed all

There was a lad with five loaves and two fishes
But that would not provide sufficient dishes
Jesus ordered the multitude to sit quietly
As he took the loaves and the fish politely

Lifting the limited food towards heaven,
He gave thanks with a heart emboldened
Lo and behold, there appeared an abundance of food
Everyone ate to their full, feeling good

After such a miraculous moment
Disciples gathered twelve baskets of food fragments
That remained after the divine feasting
That was catered for by God's blessing

Jesus' disciples were in a boat on the sea
But Jesus was not in their company
Looking out at the distant water
They perceived their master coming closer

He was walking confidently in deep water
They were shocked to witness such an encounter
Jesus said, "It is I: Do not be afraid."
Incredulously, they received Him standing in good stead.

The ability to walk on the surface of deep water
Was made possible by the invocation of divine power
Jesus used such power to defy the laws of nature
As a reminder of the power of His Father

When Jesus saw a man who was blind from birth
He anointed his eyes with spittle made from dirt
And when washed in the Siloam pool
He returned, seeing clearly and cool

Jesus and the disciples were on a ship across the deep
Tired and weary, Jesus fell asleep
A sudden storm came, putting them in great jeopardy
Water began to fill the boat rapidly

Scared and not knowing what to do
They awoke Jesus with much ado
Jesus rose and rebuked the raging wind and water
Immediately, calm and relief came together

"Where is your faith? "
Jesus asked his fellow mate.
Being in fearful doubt, they wondered.
How the wind and water as he ordered

In the country of the Gadarenes,
Jesus met a man possessed by spirits unclean
Legion begged Jesus to drive the torment out
And Jesus drove the spirits into swine running about

The awed multitude saw what was done
And they spread the great news all over town
The cured man was happy for such mercy
He published the great things in the whole city

Mary and Martha sent a message to Jesus
Saying that their brother, His friend Lazarus
Was very sick and near death
Lying in his bed, short of breath

Lazarus was pronounced dead.
Before Jesus could reach his bed
Finally, when Jesus arrived to give a remedy
Lazarus had been in the grave for four days already

Hearing such news, Jesus hurried.
To the grave where Lazarus was buried
In a loud voice, He said, "Lazarus, come forth."
And dead Lazarus arose in great comfort.

There was a woman with a blood issue for twelve years
Who couldn't get relief despite spending and tears
She came to Jesus seeking succor
Having heard of His healing power

Closely following Jesus and feeling confident.
She touched the border of His garment
Her blood issue was discontinued immediately
And Jesus asked, "Who touched me?'

His disciples reasoned aloud.
Master, it could be anyone in the crowd
"Somebody hath touched me
For I could perceive virtue is gone out of me."

When the woman realized she couldn't hide her guilt
She came forward with a trembling tilt
Falling before Jesus, she confessed
Happy for the healing that made her blessed

Jesus smiled at the woman who came forth
He said, "Daughter, be in great comfort."
Thy faith hath made the whole
Go in peace into the world

Jairus, a prominent synagogue ruler
Had asked Jesus to heal his dying daughter
But Jesus was unavoidably delayed
And so Jairus's only daughter died

Jairus said, "Master, do not trouble their heads
My daughter is now dead
Jesus said," Fear not, only believe
And your daughter will be relieved

Jesus entered the house where the dead lay
Everyone was weeping and wailing all the way
"Weep not. She is not dead, but slept."
They laughed to scorn at what He sayeth.

Jesus sent them all outside to stand
And He gently held her by the hand
Calling and saying, 'Maid, arise."
And the girl was up to everyone's surprise.

There was a man with only one son
Who the devil tore and threw down
The disciples could not cure him
Cause they lacked the miracle within

The man brought his son, whom the devil possesses
To be cured by the power of Jesus
Jesus rebuked the unclean possessive power
And delivered the cured son to his father

In a particular village in Samaria
Jesus met ten men with leprosy
They lifted their voices, seeing Jesus
"Master, have mercy upon us."

When Jesus saw them in that critical crisis
He said, "Go show yourselves unto the priest."
As they went to the priest in earnest
They were miraculously cleansed

Discovering that they were cleansed completely
One of them returned to glorify Jesus loudly
He fell on his face at Jesus' feet
Giving thanks for a saving feat

A blind man was at the wayside begging
Heard that Jesus was coming
Whence he shouted, "Jesus, have mercy on me."
Jesus said, "What wilt thou that I do unto thee?"

"Son of David, have mercy on me
Heal me so that I can see
"Receive thy sight: thy faith hath saved thee'
Immediately, he received his wish to see

Fishermen toiled all night in the Gennesaret Lake
And did not get any fish to take
They were washing their nets in a sense of failure
When Jesus requested that they go back in the water

Obediently, Simon cast his net against his wishes
Lo and behold, he caught a multitude of fishes
Everyone was astonished to witness such action
Gathering an abundance of fish with great satisfaction

Upon entry to a city in Nain
Jesus saw a widow weeping in vain
Her only son had died and was being taken away
Moved with compassion, Jesus stopped them on the way

He comforted the woman weeping in the crowd
Touching the bier, Jesus said aloud
"Youngman, I say unto you, Arise
And the dead sat up, defeating his demise

In a rowdy Jerusalem encounter
A soldier cut off Peter's right ear
Noticing Peter's plight and suffering
Jesus touched his ear for complete healing

JESUS PARABLES

A parable is a human, secular occurrence
With deep spiritual significance
Simply put, it's a short earthly story
Revealing heavenly glory

Jesus told multiple parables.
To make complex spiritual ideas understandable
He related a host of inspirational stories
To clarify, enlighten, and persuade people

Parables strengthened His teaching and ministry.
Expressing timeless wisdom effectively
Making his approach more vivid and interesting
With widespread appeal and profound meaning

Jesus employed parables not to confuse.
But to disseminate and diffuse.
Spiritual insights, truths, and love
Opening the way to the Kingdom above

Jesus recounted common, everyday experiences.
Daily scenarios in family, society, and business
Challenging listeners to think logically
And to apply inherent lessons personally

Jesus skillfully compared the unseen and the unfamiliar.
With what was mundane and familiar
He revealed sacred secrets to God's Kingdom
Expressing various forms of intentional wisdom

He told parables not as an art of entertainment
Or a lifeless lecture of benign bewilderment
His parables were not based on logical argumentation
But based on the power of persuasion

A confident man going from Jerusalem to Jericho
Was robbed, beaten, and left in limbo
A priest saw him but passed by
A Levite saw him but left him to die

A good Samaritan came by and saw him
In pity, he helped him and took him to an Inn
And he paid all the expenses
For him to regain his health and his senses

The parable of the good Samaritan
Demonstrates neighborly kindness and compassion
Extending love not only to the next-door neighbor
But to your enemy, outsider and stranger

Behold, a Sower went forth to sow seeds
Some seeds fell on the wayside indeed
Fowls and birds ate them out
Having no chance to spring or sprout

Some fell on hollow grounds and withered
Others fell among thorns and were smothered
Some fell on good, fertile ground
And became productive all year round

Different soils represent different ears and hearts
Of folks and believers who receive what God imparts
Some folks disdain and disregard
Others receive, digest, and drive forward

The Sower is the Son of God
The soil is the world made by the Lord
The good seeds are the children of His Kingdom
The distractions and dangers are weapons of Satan

Behold, a son asked his father for his share of the wealth
To live a riotous life that threatened his health
Broke, he had to work as a servant feeding pigs
Hungry and desperate, he ate the swine husks and twigs

Coming to his senses, he returned to his father
Asking for forgiveness and a job as a stranger
Father welcomed him with a redemptive compliment
Dressed him for a feast and a reunion merriment

This parable reveals God's immense love and willingness
Offering repentant sinners, a new life and forgiveness
The prodigal was lost but was found
Repenting and returning to happy, holy ground

The grain of mustard seed is the smallest
When it was sown, it grew and became the largest
Similarly, the greatness of God's Kingdom starts small initially
With firm faith, it can grow and expand exponentially

Parables of lost sheep and lost coin illustrate
The efforts and perseverance the losers demonstrate
At recovery, redemption is taken to the limit
Resulting in rejoicing to regain it

Similarly, God becomes impatient when sinners are lost
To satanic trends and tendencies at all costs
But when they repent and return to Him
He forgives and rejoices with a grin

Jesus' parables and lessons
Are likened to the Kingdom of Heaven
The five virgins were prepared to enter
But the five foolish ones were shut out forever

Armed with oil in lamps to give light
The five wise virgins met the bridegroom at midnight
The five foolish virgins with no oil in their lamp
Failed and floundered in the dark and damp

Behold, the rich fool built bigger barns
To stow his bountiful crops from his farms
Boasting "I have great abundance to live in ease and delight."
Not knowing that he would die that night.

The lesson here is to be wary of graspingness
Man's life doesn't consist of the things he possesses
Do not lay treasure upon yourself lavishly
But be rich in God and live righteously

Jesus likened his faithful followers to a wise man
Who built his house on rock, not sand
The house withstood storms and did not fall
Because its foundation steadied and stood tall

The foolish man built his house on sand
When the storm came, it fell flat on the land
Demonstrating that feeble and fragmented faith
Will not take you to the heavenly gate

Jesus' parables capture and involve earthly experiences
Of human beings in a variety of circumstances
No reference made to animals or inanimate objects
Showing His care, love, and dedication to human subjects

His parables presented perspectives and possibilities.
Generating gateways and opening opportunities
For humanity to accept and adhere to His teachings
Of spiritual insights, love, forgiveness, and righteous living

JESUS MINISTRY

Jesus' ministry, teachings, and oracle
There were more than parables, sermons, and miracles
He devoted His entire ministry
To love, forgive, obey, and be humble

His life, work, words, and deeds
Purposefully planted fertile seeds
That inspires and influence our lives
With eternal truths on which to strive

His core teaching rested on the love of God
Our Creator and provident Lord
Loving Him with all your heart, mind, and soul
And giving gratitude for blessings that unfold

He taught us to obey God's rule and righteousness
To repent for sins and seek His forgiveness
And have firm faith in God's infinite power
To enter His Kingdom forever

Jesus emphasized the love of thy neighbor
The person near you or the stranger
The goodness you show and share to bring them relief
Will multiply and magnify beyond belief

Jesus personal life and earthly examples
Exemplify selfless service and moral principles
And demonstrating compassion, care, and remedy
To all, especially the sick, poor, and needy

Jesus lessons of love venerate virtue.
"Love your enemies, bless them that curse you."
Do good to them that hurt you
And pray for those who despise and persecute you

Love your neighbor as yourself.
Basically, we are good to ourselves.
Jesus tells us to extend similar love
And blessings will flow from above

The love that Jesus preached and personified
Has the divine, dynamic power to defy
All hatred, hurt, hindrance, and horror
And overcome obstacles, disappointment, and sorrow

Jesus placed a premium and paramount power
On love and its capacity, capability, and caliber
Ascribing to it definitive and dignified dexterity
That impacts hearts with indescribable invincibility

Jesus looked upon love as the key to God's Kingdom
A deliverance from darkness to the light of wisdom
A liberation from the clutches and traps of Satan
And the redemption from sins and limitation

Love is demonstrated in three dimensions.
In thoughts, feelings, and actions
Jesus thought and felt deeply for people with low incomes and the needy
Healing the sick, feeding the hungry, and raising the dead people

He taught us to think well of our neighbor
Feeling empathy, sympathy, and care for those who suffer
Do good and kind deeds to a stranger
Always show love to thyself and one another

Instead of a tooth for a tooth and an eye for an eye"
Strive to elevate each other to a glorious high
Love has no room for revenge or retaliation
True love forgives and forgets, seeking no compensation

Greed and lust diminish love's power.
Learn to look out for and respect one another
Envy and jealousy destroy love's foundation
Don't covet or compare in any situation

Faith is the belief in God, the Creator
Steadfast, firm faith can accomplish whatever
You desire a decent, devotional goal.
"Be of good comfort, thy faith hath made the whole."

Cultivate charity and give alms secretly.
Not hypocritically or openly for all to see
God does not reward showmanship in acts of philanthropy
"Thy Father, which is in secret, shall reward thee openly."

Forgiveness is a profound pillar in the preaching of Jesus
The remarkable ability to forgive those who trespass
The courage to forgive seventy times seven
Producing relief and blessings from Heaven

Forgiveness is medicine for the body.
A remedy for emotional pain and anxiety
It's the succor that soothes the soul
Bringing clarity and freedom to the mind untold

Jesus warned us about storing treasure on earth
Heart and mind are consumed in protecting its worth
Direct your mind and soul to Heavenly treasures
To open the divine door to spiritual pleasures

Let not your heart be troubled over today or tomorrow
Be independent and soar like the sparrow
First seek the Kingdom of God and His righteousness
He will fulfill your needs by His mercy and faithfulness

God has empowered Mother Nature.
To cater to the needs of every creature
Fish in the water, birds in the air, animals in the main
And man at the top of the food chain

Judge not, that ye be not judged
Tit for tat, just smear and smudge
First, fix your faults and wrongs
Before attempting to condemn others headlong

Be careful what the mouth speaketh
It can create trouble beyond regret
In speech, be brief and accurate.
Knowing when silence is appropriate.

If you humbly ask or seek something
It will eventually avail itself without failing
Positive answers and goodness shall come
As a result of your good deeds done

There is no shame in asking for favors
And no gain in remaining shy forever
Ask in a polite, affable manner
And people will surely deliver

Whatever goes into a man's mouth
Does not defile him without a doubt
But that which cometh from the mouth of man
Is responsible for defiling man

Never criticize any culture of consumption.
Or carp on the kinds of food people live on
Their goodness of heart and mind are let out
By deeds and words of mouth

Jesus taught us to protect peace and the purity of the soul
And not be attached to worldly gains or goals
Beauty and blessings come from the sanctity of the soul
Don't compromise or exchange it for temporary gold

Jesus extolled the innocence and humility of children
Be converted and become like little children to enter Heaven
Don't offend anyone, minimal ones
To live without woes and reprimands

If your brother trespasses against Thee
Tell him about his fault in privacy
If he listens and makes amends, you gain compensation
If he refuses, seek counseling or congregational intervention

What God hath put together
Let no man put asunder
When men leave their mother and father
They cleave to their wives and become one figure

The emphasis on the accumulation of wealth and possession
It represents a deadly distraction from salvation
Easier for a camel to go through the eye of a needle
Than for a rich man to enter God's cradle

Those who forsake materialism and family
And have given everything to people experiencing poverty, and follow me
Shall inherit everlasting life
And forever be saved from stress and strife

Jesus said all things shall come to believers
What they sincerely ask for in prayers
Be bold and steadfast in believing
And be ready to receive the rich blessings

Believe in me and keep my commandments
I'll pray for your comfort and contentment
I'll prepare a place for you in my Father's Mansion
I'm the way, the truth, and the life towards salvation

The Spirit of the Lord within Me
Seeking to help poor and sick people
"I come not to call on the righteous
I come to save sinners and the unrighteous

Jesus preached peace in all shades and grades
Let's not let your heart be troubled or afraid
Abide in me and I in you
My peace and love I give to you.

ATTRIBUTES OF JESUS

Jesus is the hallowed hallmark of humility
His lowly birth in a manger is a telling testimony
Beginning in the humblest of homes
Meekly modest on straw and stones

Rather than being served, Jesus served people
He raised the dead and healed the sick openly
He taught, led, and fed large crowds
And never took credit or felt unduly proud

His humility rose to the pinnacle at Passover
Serving supper to his disciples in a subservient manner
Then, washing their feet at His own free will
And dry them with a towel

Jesus was indeed bountifully blessed.
With a mountain of meekness and gentleness
He was not brash, bombastic, or belligerent
He glorified childish love and innocence

Jesus is a sanctified symbol of simplicity
Having limited clothing, wooden sandals, and no cosmetology
No mansion, no bank account, no car, no plane
Just living a life, pure and plain

Fed on natural food, not any sophisticated diet
Giving God thanks, then eating in quiet

Not worshipping in a mega chapel or cathedral
Constantly offering sincere prayers without regal ritual

His teaching was simple, not complicated or complex
Pontificating peacefully, not from a script or any text
His oral delivery was straightforward and understandable
Punctuating his preaching with pertinent parables

Mindfulness moved and manipulated his ministry.
Mercy and compassion characterized his homily.
Placating people with low incomes, nourishing people in need, and healing sufferers
Saving sinners, giving life, loving and serving others

His generosity is gargantuan and genuine.
Willingly sacrificing time, talent, effort divine
His masterpiece of generosity was given on the gallows
Where He lay down his life for friends and foes

Jesus is the faithful Father of forgiveness
Forgiving sinners, enemies in complete earnestness
He taught the virtues and rewards of forgiving
Forgive, and you shall be forgiven

He forgave Judas, the worthless kisser.
Who betrayed Him for thirty pieces of silver
A betrayal that delivered His death
Yet He did forgive and forget

His most significant act of forgiveness that nothing can surpass
Was His utterance whilst dying on the cross
"Father, forgive them, for they know not what they do
Pardoning his killers for the sake of me and you

Jesus was a maestro and a monument of patience
Devoutly demonstrated dignified diligence
During His entire ministry, service and offers
To His disciples and all His followers

Showing profound patience to the multitude and gatherings
Listening to their woes, solving problems, and enduring long suffering
Expending time, tolerance, teaching faith and Godliness
Tarrying, talking, and walking in graceful gladness

To God, Jesus offered overwhelming obedience.
God comes first in all His deeds and deliverance
Being rigorously righteous, following commandments with ease
Resulted in "This is My Son in whom I am well pleased. "

Jesus was a paramount paragon of peace
His birth glorified Advent as a peaceful centerpiece
He advocated and recommended a peaceful resolution
To all conflict, crises, friction, and contention

His principal purpose rested on peace and goodwill
To all men on earth under God's will
Preaching on the pertinence and path to peace
That's doable, sustainable, and within reach

My peace I give to the sisters and brothers
Go in peace and serve one another
If you're slapped, turn the other cheek
Retaliation brings havoc, bloody and bleak

Jesus is the titanic transformation of truth
His utterances and actions produced flawless fruits
Always praising and honoring God for His achievement
And never to honor Himself for His accomplishment

He shuns lies and liars.
And never lied to His persecutors.
He steadfastly stuck to the truth and honesty
A tremendous testimony to truth taken to Calvary

Seek and know the truth in Me
And the truth shall make you free
Jesus treated truth as a religion in itself
Pursue and practice it to elevate and save thyself

Jesus was a trailblazer and a role model of self-control
Hardly reacting provocatively or aggressively to any soul
Never cursed the Jews or Gentiles nor the Pharisees
Who questioned His authority and denigrated His dignity

He did not punish Peter for denying Him
He still loved and served Judas after he betrayed Him
He didn't harshly discipline His disciples
For not having faith in His power and principles

OUR GRATITUDE TO JESUS

We owe and must show gratitude to Jesus
For gems of wisdom and a moral compass
To live our lives with a divine purpose
Faithful, honorable, righteous, and gracious

Be thankful for His lessons of unconditional love
For your neighbor, self, and the father above
His love is a radical power and miracle
Capable of making each of us a dignified disciple

We're grateful to Jesus for the "Our Father " prayer.
Delivered in His sermon on the Mount to followers
A prayer that is said daily by billions of people
In homes, churches, cathedrals, and chapels

The Lord's prayer is offered in educational institutions
Globally, from kindergarten to tertiary foundation
An all-inclusive prayer, solemn and short
Readily recited from the depths of the heart

We're grateful for the goodness of the Golden Rule
A decent, dignified principle devoid of ridicule
Treating others the way you want to be treated
His message for peaceful co-existence is undiluted

Grateful to Him for being a righteous role model
Setting superlative examples, humble and simple
Illumination, inspiration, and navigational amplitudes
To adopt acts and attitudes appropriate for altitude

Grateful for His demonstration of the power of gratitude
Marvelously mandating the miracle of magnitude
First, giving genuine thanks to God with relish
For five loaves of bread and two fish

Appreciate His warning of wolves in sheep's clothing
Knowing the world is full of trickery and cheating
Be wise as serpents and gentle as doves
And be guided by divine direction from above

Thank you for telling us to send Caesar his due
And to God, praise and worship from you
Fulfill your earthly and daily obligations
Balanced and blessed by spiritual devotion

Value His advice to honor your parents
So that your days will be long and abundant
We owe our lives to our parents
Who nurture and mold us towards independence

We're grateful for His reminder to be obedient
To all of God's laws and Commandments
Spiritual as well as secular guides and policy
Providing and protecting peace, safety, and sanctity

Grateful for His instruction to have abiding faith
In God for strength and refuge, solid and straight
Laying up our treasures in Heaven
And not to be manipulated by material burden

Thankful for His sermon on selfless service
Rising above selfishness, ego, pride, and prejudice
Knowing that greatness comes from serving others
And not from exploiting them for profit or plunder

Grateful for His positive impact on humanity
Being the cause and creation of Christianity
The largest, most popular religion
With believers and followers in every nation

Christ's flesh empowers us through thick and thin
His blood washes away all our sins
His words give us a purposeful perspective
Impacting our lives with a transformative objective

Grateful for His guidance to always keep your word
Be truthful and brief, not artless and absurd
Honor promises and pledges you espouse
Towards friends, family, co-workers, and spouses

Thankful for His admonition to let your light shine
Revealing your fruits that are sinless and divine
Built on constant, sincere prayers and pious prudence
Good deeds, charity, and repentance

Grateful for His caution not to criticize or condemn
Not to judge, belittle, discredit, or malign
To promote peace, praise, and prosperity
Not controversy, conflict, tension, nor animosity

THE TRIUMPHANT ENTRY

Faithfully following Jesus' instruction
Two disciples went out to get nature's transportation
An ass and a colt, surefooted and solemn
On which Jesus rode into Jerusalem

Jesus deliberately rode in on a donkey
To symbolize simplicity, purity, and humility
He did not enter on a war horse or a stately steed
Which represented force or royal breed

He intentionally wore the clothes of the poor
Not expensive, classy ones that the rich endure
Riding in not as a conqueror by force of soldiery
But as a conqueror by love, grace, and mercy

His message and mission as the Messiah
To win hearts and minds as the Saviour
Not boasting as an earthly King in a temporal Palace
But the King of Peace in a spiritual Palace

A great multitude gladly welcomed Him that day
By willingly spreading their garments on the way
Some strew branches from palm trees
Subsequently observed as Palm Sunday for Thee

When the crowd saw Jesus entering the city
They were moved with marvel and curiosity
Wanting to know "Who is this? "
The Prophet from Nazareth was named Jesus.

Shouting on top of their breadth
"Blessed is He that cometh
In the name of the Lord, Hosanna in the Highest."
Marking His triumphant entry to Jerusalem, bold and blessed

Not pleased with the system of government
They needed leadership to resist oppressive treatment
So, they greeted Jesus as the revolutionary leader
Who would challenge and change the emperor

Perceiving Jesus as the new King of the Jews
Believing that the Messiah embraced radical views
To effect socio-economic and political changes
They hailed Him as the hero on high hinges

Realizing that Jesus was not the warlike revolutionary
But a Saviour winning hearts with love and placidity
They made a 360-degree turn for the worse
That brought on His crucifixion curse

Jesus went straight to God's temple.
And drove out the vendors and businesspeople
Overthrowing the tables and seats
Used by the den of thieves and hypocrites

Jesus's renunciation of business ventures in the church
It is an indication to separate religion from commerce
Man's emphasis on materialism over spirituality
Opens avenues to depravity and immorality

Pursuit of pleasures and possessions
And ill-gotten gains from capitalist concoction
Defiled the church and religious order
And breed all brands of breaches and blunders

In Jerusalem, Jesus continued preaching and healing
And this left the priests and elders wondering
By whose authority was he doing miraculous things
Jesus just confused them with parabolic renderings

From conception, Jesus was blessed with intelligence
Knowledge and wisdom granted by Providence
He utilized it in every context and circumstance
To teach and preach with confidence and clairvoyance

The Priests and Pharisees in their wickedness
Tried to corner and entangle Jesus
Asking, "Is it lawful to give tribute to Caesar or not?"
Jesus shrewd answers surprised and hurt them a lot.

Seeing the image on the tribute money
He offered the fundamental testimony
Render to Caesar the things that are Caesar's
And unto God the things that are God's

In Jerusalem, Jesus warned us about wars
Nations rising against nations near and far
The world will face problems and afflictions
And the end rests in God's jurisdiction

Jesus' prediction of armed conflict came true
Currently, wars are wreaking havoc all over
The centuries from then to today
With no end in sight until Doomsday

The arms race leads to the stockpiling of weapons
Engineered by a lack of trust and respect among nations
Competition, greed, injustice, and pride
Give way to confrontation, casualties, and genocide

He urged us to be good beings of God's creation
Despite countless trials and tribulations
And after the world is darkened and shaken
He will come again from the clouds of Heaven

TRANSFIGURATION

With earnest expectation and spiritual vigor
Jesus led Peter, James, and John to Mount Tabor
To a special, secluded, and hallowed place
Where a pivotal, profound phenomenon would take place

Becoming tired of the arduous ascent
The disciples fell asleep at the last moment
But were rudely awakened
Majestically created by Jesus' transfiguration

Shocked, they expressed their fear aloud.
As they were overshadowed by a big, bright cloud
They saw Jesus in the company of two men
In a snow-white garment covering them

They beheld Jesus in great wonderment.
Being transfigured in a dazzling white garment
A telltale theology of total radiance
A unique, unsurpassed revelation of resplendence

Jesus had a conversation with Moses and Elijah
Concerning his impending departure
They were discussing Jesus' crucifixion and resurrection
And his ascribed, ultimate Ascension

The disciples heard a voice from heaven coming down
Saying "This is my beloved Son."
Listen to Him: hear Him.
The disciples' faith in Jesus is affirmed therein.

The heavenly voice confirmed that Jesus is the Son of God
A powerful point was accepted with much applause
Substantiated by the return of Elijah and Moses
A monumental moment with significant emphasis

Transfiguration represents a Trinitarian revelation.
God speaking from heavenly elevation
Son of God in all His glittering glory
And the Holy Spirit was captured in the cloud's beauty

Moses represents the Mosaic Law
The Law God gave Moses without flaw
Elijah symbolizes the fulfillment of the Prophets
Through which Christianity reaped many benefits

The actualization of Jesus' transfiguration
Represents a potent and pivotal prong of Christian tradition
A monumental meeting of divinity and humanity
Of temporal tendencies and spiritual supremacy

Transfiguration signifies the inevitable connection.
Of heaven and earth in constant motion
One cannot exist and function without the other
They are ordered and orchestrated to work together

Essentially, the transfiguration is a testimony to purity
Clean, white, dazzling robes of divinity
The presiding power and presence of the Almighty
Superimposed on secular reality

Transfiguration is the temporal theophany.
Where Mother Earth endears God's mercy
A dynamic dichotomy of spiritual and secular forces
With a self-possessed signature of significant sources

Jesus' transfiguration can be seen.
As a profound preparatory lesson
For Jesus to pay the precious price
As the virtuous victim making the ultimate sacrifice

TRIAL OF JESUS

Days before the Feast of Passover
Jesus told His disciples a truth, sad and somber
The Son of man will be betrayed and crucified
A death that's divinely prescribed and sanctified

Disciples complained about a woman's willful waste
Of pouring expensive oil on Jesus' head and face
But Jesus glorified the goodness of such a ritual
Saying that, the woman did it for his burial

After that, a disciple called Judas Iscariot
Went to the chief priest and hatched a plot
He promised to deliver
Jesus for thirty pieces of silver

Jesus knew that Judas would do this
And betray the Son of God with a kiss
Just before Jesus' trial did begin
Judas walked up to Jesus and kissed Him

Envy and jealousy are weaknesses of character
They build and breed designs and desire
To bring down and betray man and country
Just for the love of money

The chief Priest and elders came forward
Arrested Jesus and tried Him in Annas courtyard

Seeing this, His disciples forsook Him and fled
Revealing the inherent weaknesses humanity bred

Just before this, Peter boasted about his loyalty
To Jesus, whom he had followed faithfully
In Messianic expectation and predictive power
Jesus remarked, "You will deny me three times, Peter."

As Jesus was tried in the chief priest's courtyard
Peter sat in the crowd, fearful and breathing hard
Confronted thrice in an accusing thrust
That he was a friend and follower of Jesus

A servant girl said, "Thou was with Jesus of Galilee."
Denying Peter said, "I know not what you say to me."
Another said, "This fellow was with Jesus of Nazareth."
Again, Peter denied Jesus in bold breadth

Another said, "Surely you are one of them
Because your speech betrays you to the helm
Peter cursed and swore at them in shrew
And immediately the cock crew

At that timely moment
Peter remembered Jesus' words of prophetic content
In remorse, he went outside and wept bitterly
Evidence of his weakness and frailty

From Anna's courtyard, Jesus was led to the chief priest Caiaphas
The elders sought false witness against Jesus

Desperately wanting to put Him to death
Saying that Jesus posed a serious threat

Despite false evidence brought by the witness
Nothing was found against Jesus
Pressured to admit that he was the Son of God
Resulted in blasphemy and death, too bad

The claim that Jesus was the Son of God
In the chief priest's kangaroo court of fraud
Caused him to be very angry, ripping his clothes
And to pronounce judgment of deathly blows

Jesus was accused of destroying the temple
And rebuilding it in three days, straight and simple
They testified that this was an act of mutiny
Not knowing that Jesus was referring to His body

With the fabrication and false charges at the religious trial
Jewish elders and Priests sealed Jesus' death as final
But they had no executive power
So, they concocted a civil trial headed by the Governor

After Caiaphas pronounced Jesus guilty
The mob treated Jesus with gross indignity
They spat in His face and smote Him with their hands
Which Jesus silently suffered without reprimands

Such humiliation, indignity, and calamity
Products of partiality, perjury, and falsity

Continue to plague the world we live in
And festers when good men do nothing

Witnessing developments, Judas returned the silver.
To the chief Priest and elders
He repented that he played the betrayal game
And went away and hanged himself, ashamed

Caiaphas and the Sanhedrin led Jesus in dishonor
And delivered Him to Pontius Pilate, the Governor
Who listened to the false allegations against Jesus
And found that Jesus was guiltless

Jesus had listened to all the accusations against Him
Noted the fabrication, conspiracies, and lies therein
But he kept a solemn silence in serenity
Insomuch that the Governor marveled greatly

Jesus was taken to King Herod.
Who found no fault in the Son of God
And He was brought back to Pontius Pilate
Who gave in to the crowd's demand for Jesus' death

As was customary during the Passover feast
One prisoner was to get the Governor's release
Whom do you want me to set free at last
Jesus, who is called Christ or Barabbas

The crowd chose convicted criminal Barabbas.
Instead of innocent Christ Jesus

Pilate knew their mischief in their hearts
Wanting to denounce and tear Him apart

Pilate asked them what to do with Jesus, the victim
And they all shouted, "Crucify him."
The Governor said, "I found no evil in this man."
Vociferously, the crowd repeated its crucifixion demand.

Disappointed, Pilate realized he could prevail at nothing
Gave in to their demands just to prevent any rioting
Washing his hands before them for good reason
Saying "I'm innocent of the blood of this just person."

True justice is denied or delayed.
When adjudicators become flawed and debased
Bowing to self-preservation and personal redress
And to public pressure and political correctness

Accepting Jesus' blood on themselves and their descendants
Pilate released Barabbas and delivered the Lamb of innocence
Soldiers seized and stripped Jesus in a common hall
Then they put on Him a purple overall

They belittled and mocked Him without dread
As they put a crown of thorns upon His head
Their mocking and hitting were painful and profuse
Saying "Hail, the King of the Jews "

Soldiers replaced the overall with His own garment
And led Him away to the Golgotha pavement

Jesus bore His cross towards the crucifixion ground
And was ably assisted by a Cyrenaic named Simon

A great crowd followed Jesus to Calvary
Some laughed loathsomely, others lamented in sympathy
Hearing the bewailing and weeping of women
Jesus said, "Weep not for me, but yourselves and children."

Walking on the way of sorrow and sacrifice to Calvary
Along the lamentable lane of mourning and mockery
The monumental and memorial march to martyrdom
Which ultimately opened the door to Christendom

To Mary, holy Mother of Christ Jesus
Following her Son to His end was a must
Sacredly, stolidly, she showed stamina
To follow Jesus to His grave in Golgotha

Magnified and blessed since Her Annunciation
Inspired and instructed in the iconic Incarnation
She knew and accepted the fate of her beloved Son
Making the ultimate sacrifice for sinners on the run

With the last words and look at His Mother's temple
He entrusted her to the care of the disciple
Then came the sacred separation, pitiful and painful
Borne by Mother and Son in submission, abiding and awful

We do not know and cannot tell for sure
About the parting pain, Mother and So endure

We can't imagine the depth of torture and agony
But can share their sorrow with empathy and sympathy

At Calvary, soldiers nailed Jesus to the cross
They parted His garments, cast lots, and tossed
Then mounted Jesus between Earth and Heaven
With the "THIS IS THE KING OF THE JEWS" inscription

Despite His torture and sorrow, Jesus said without ado
"Father, forgive them; for they know not what they do. "
Priests and elders mocked Him, saying to themselves
"He saved others, but He cannot save Himself. "

Two thieves shared a similar sacrificial plight
One hung on His left and one on His right
Recognizing Jesus innocence, one asked Jesus to remember him
When unto Heaven He is risen

Taking brutality brazenly beyond the brink
They gave Jesus vinegar laced with gall to drink
After tasting it, he refused to swallow
Such ignoble and insulting brew in sorrow

Not wanting bodies on the cross on the Sabbath
Pilate's permission was besought
To quicken the death of the condemned on the cross
By breaking their legs, piercing their sides at all costs

The soldiers broke the legs of the two thieves
Who shuddered and shouted to death without ease
They did not cut Jesus' leg because He was already dead
They pierced His side with a spear instead

Out came from His wound blood and water
In fulfillment of the holy Scripture
Not a bone in His body shall be broken
Just the wound to let out the saving blood from Heaven

The crucifixion is the consecrated culmination in Christianity
Upholding the ultimate sacrifice as the critical climax at Calvary
Which sanctified and sealed the victory of Jesus
Of life over death, heavenly haul over earthly terminus

Jesus, the saint, submitted to the sacrificial suffering
Laying down His life as a fateful feat of forgiving
People for their sins and wrongdoing
A monumental mark of deliverance and blessing

The cross symbolizes and signifies a significant sacrifice
A righteous and ritual reminder of the precious price
Jesus paid at Calvary for our salvation
Willingly and without regret or reservation

Whilst Jesus was dying on the cross in innocence
Heaven and earth responded in resistance
Strange and loud noises descended from the sky
And the earth shook in a violent reply

In shame and sadness, the Sun sank into darkness
Joining in the oracular outcry against unrighteousness
This heavenly and earthly reaction to the crucifixion
Demonstrated God's authority in a sad situation

Jesus' crucifixion was a devout demonstration.
Of God's appearance on earth as a human manifestation
Righteously revealing His deep, unconditional love for us
Coming as the Son of Man, called Jesus

The crucifixion and resurrection of Jesus
Must be the constant reminder to all of us
We are all created in the image of God
Blood and flesh representation and extension of God

Jesus was nailed to the cross, hanging
Showing that good over evil involves suffering
He willingly gave His life to save us
So, live righteously before you cross to join Jesus

Crucifixion showed how far Jesus went.
To save humanity that's hell-bent
It offers reprieve, relief, and a release
From trials, tribulations, and spiritual disease

Then came darkness on land all over
From the sixth to the ninth hour
People heard Jesus call on Elias openly
"My God, my God, why hast Thou forsaken me?"

The sun stopped shining, and the Earth shaken
And the temple was split wide open
"Father, into Thy hands I commend my spirit."
Having said that, Jesus kicked the bucket.

Jesus knew about his betrayal, denial, and crucifixion
Being part of prophecy and Messianic expectation
He didn't use divine powers to avoid the adventure
Because they must be done in fulfillment of the Scripture

Goodness and greatness carry a signature of sacrifice
Produced and propagated by a precious price
Anything of significance, substance, and salvation
Proceed from the trademark of trials and tribulations

The Holy Week marks the acceptance and rejection of Jesus
The triumphant entry quickly turned to cultural chaos
A critical clash of religious and civil forces
Foreshadowed, foretold by prophesied directives

The revelation and realities of Holy Week
The rushed trials, warped and weak
Exposed the limitations and frailties of human nature
And the manifestation of God's authority and power

The significance of Holy Week is surpassed
By the beauty and blessings of Advent and Christmas
Both signify and represent the paramount pillars
Of Christianity and its spiritual splendor

INRI

JESUS ON THE CROSS

The cross is the symbol of sacrifice
Upon which Jesus paid the ultimate price
It represents the final signature of His last breadth
A slow, excruciatingly painful death

The crucifixion of Jesus Christ at Calvary
Represents God's unconditional love and mercy
And Jesus' suffering love for human beings
Willingly paying the penalty for our sins

The cross is a symbol of victory
Overcoming sins and spiritual bankruptcy
A victory of life over death
Where resurrection delivers a new breadth

The cross reveals a new life for us
An opportunitywith renewed purpose
The crucifixion was not the end or closure
But a call to believers to seek Jesus' cover

The cross bridges the gap between God and humanity
A crucial confluence of the worldly and spirituality
Where divine justice and mercy
Made manifest in all its glory

The Lamb of God was sacrificed on the cross
It was perfect, unblemished, and without gloss

Where blessed blood was shed in solemnity
For the forgiveness and redemption of humanity

Hanging heavily on a huge cross
It was indeed a pitiful, painful physical loss
Spiritually, it was a propitious price paid
Jesus on the cross languishly laid

Showing no reluctance or resistance
Jesus bore His cross in due diligence
A merciful and monumental mission
For man's deliverance and remission

On the cross, He silently suffered solo
Under the iniquity of men bent so low
He endured the pangs and pain
Created by man's injustice and disdain

His cross is the symbol of saving face
The crucifix of salvation and grace
Holy and hallowed by God's love
Our merciful Father above

In solidarity with such a seminal sacrifice
Where Jesus paid the consummate price
Man must take up his cross
In self-denial and devotion to Jesus

The cross represents the immortal intersection.
Of God's love and mercy and mankind's transgression

The perpendicular portion is God's righteous ransom
The horizontal hold is man's iniquitous prong.

THE AFTERMAUTH

Joseph of Arimathea, Jesus's close crony.
Begged Pilate for Jesus dead body
Which he wrapped in a clean linen cloth
And laid it in a tomb he had wrought

The chief priests and Pharisees sought permission
To secure Jesus' body and avoid any machination
By the disciples to show that Jesus is risen
Three days after I got to the sepulcher prison

They went and secured the sepulcher for sure
By placing a huge rock at the door
And paid soldiers to keep watch
Making sure that Jesus' body wasn't snatched

Mary and others came to the sepulcher on the Sabbath spell
Behold, they saw the rock rolled back by an angel
The angelic presence and powers
Shook and silenced all the gatekeepers

The angel addressed the women, "Don't be terrified."
I know you seek Jesus, who was crucified
He showed them the empty tomb where the Lord laid
Telling them that Jesus hath risen from the dead

They were directed by an Angel
To go quickly and to tell.

His disciples that He is risen from the dead
And He would meet them in Galilee instead

Hurriedly, they departed from the sepulcher.
With great joy, fear, and fervor
To bring good news to His disciples
Of His resurrection miracle

Embarking on this noble mission without fail
Behold, Jesus met them, saying, "All hail."
And they came and held Him by His feet
Worshipping Him in a joyful greet

Jesus told them to notify His disciples
That He would see them in Galilee, His home circle
Obediently, the disciples went to the appointed place
And there they saw Jesus in full face

When the disciples saw Jesus appearing
They were bewildered, surprised by this happening
Skeptical, doubtful of something so miraculous
Cautiously, they approached and felt the flesh of Jesus

'Jesus is alive,' declared the disciples to Thomas
Doubtful Thomas refused to believe such trash
Except I see the nail prints on His hands
And the spear wound in His rib bands

After eight days, Jesus appeared in front of Thomas
"Peace be unto you. Hold my hands at last.

Thrust them into my side.
Feel my body with faithful pride.

Thomas was happily surprised.
To see and feel his Master alive
And he said, "My Lord and my God."
Not doubting anymore, but believing in the Lord.

Convinced that Jesus was alive
Happy over the death, he did survive
They bowed down and worshipped Him gloriously
Knowing that Jesus' prophecy was manifested truly

He blessed them with the power of incarnate authority
To get out in the world and spread Christianity
Teaching and baptizing people
In the name of the Holy Trinity

The wondrous works of the Holy Week revealed
And established the birthing grounds unsullied
The fundamental foundation of a religion
That touched and is reaching all nations

The epic episode of Christ Jesus
Is recorded in a religious robust
In the New Testament of the Holy Bible
The consecrated cornerstone, chaste and credible

The life and works of Chris Jesus
Became the impressive, immense impetus

That evangelizes, energizes, and elevates individuals
With positive transformation, critical and colossal

Believing and adopting Jesus' teachings
Not only enrich and transform Earthlings
But provides a moral compass and fortification
Against iniquities, trials, and tribulations

Searching for simplicity, seek Jesus.
Hungry for humility, hang on to Jesus
Chasing chastity and candor call on Jesus
Looking for love and peace, trust Jesus

To overcome temptation and greed, count on Christ
In trouble, affliction, and disappointment, lean on Jesus
Broken, disheartened, and despondent people rely on Jesus
Unemployed, poor, neglected, commit to Christ

THE PENTECOST

In the Bible, Joel and Ezekiel foretold
That the day of Pentecost would unfold
The descent and dynamics of the Holy Spirit
Unto the world in a timely visit

The day of Pentecost arrived at the appointed hour
Fifty days after the Feast of Passover
As Jesus did promise His disciples
The power of the Holy Spirit in their circles

Pentecost is the outpouring of God's Spirit
Creating renewed hearts and new spirits
Within His people of all nations
Replacing hearts of stone and transgression

Anticipated many times by Jesus
That the Holy Spirit would dwell among us
Empowering us as a unified, renewed Body
With love-filled power and spiritual sanctity

Pentecost was a powerful phenomenon.
Happening in the heart of Jerusalem
Where disciples and a large crowd gathered
People of all flocks and diverse feathers

They were of one accord in one place
When Pentecost did take place

Suddenly, there came a sound from heaven
As of rushing, mighty wind

It filled the house where they were sitting
There appeared cloven tongues firing
Upon each of them beginning to speak differently
As the Spirit afforded such facility

They were all filled with the Holy Ghost
Amazed and marveled in a multilingual boast
Everyone in their own tongue of laud
Spoke and understood the wonderful works of God

The disciples and followers were in a party mood
Loudly and cheerfully chatting, chanting, and feeling good
Onlookers thought they were all drunk
A presumption that Peter did debunk

Saying that it was too early to get drunk
These men were engrossed in a spiritual moment
Filled and powered by the Holy Ghost
And not engaged in any drinking toast

Peter reminded them of the Biblical prophecy
That the Holy Spirit would descend upon everybody
Sons and daughters shall prophesy
Older men dream, and young men see visions

Pentecost represents the fulfillment of prophecy.
Made for the future growth of Christianity

The rebirth, renewal, and spiritual upliftment
Of Christians spread under God's firmament

Pentecost portends the powerful convergence.
Of divine design, Spiritual spread, and secular acceptance
God sends the Holy Spirit in the midst of humanity
With love and gospel guidance growing in spirituality

Having the spiritual strength to transform lives
Breathing better in all our daily dives
In different circumstances and diverse realities
Riding the blessed bandwagon of Christianity

Pentecost is the powerful reset button.
To shun sins and seek pardon.
Through the Holy Ghost and Father in heaven
Whose grace can ease all of your burden

Proudly put on your Pentecostal apparition.
Empowered by gospel compulsion
To dream, desire, and deserve deliverance
Into the Holy Hands of the Creator's credence

Pentecost gives Christians the moral mileage.
Spreading the word of God to every country, town, and village
Trending on the testimonies of tongues, diverse and deep
With the Holy Spirit as the Shepherd of the sheep

The power of Pentecost penetrates every continent
Inspiring and influencing the lives of every recipient

From the shores of South America and North America
To the lands in Europe, Australia, Africa, and Asia

Nothing can stop the tidal waves of the Pentecost
Coming fifty days after a sacrificial cost
To move man mercifully through trials and tribulations
To the location of lasting love, hope, and salvation.

Be awash and aware of the power of Pentecost
Let it be the divine energy to propel you at all costs
Be a participant in its mystery and glory
Celebrating its presence, purpose, and piety

Allow the Holy Spirit to work wonders in you
As an integral part of the Cosmic glue
Let it be the Light to dispel darkness
And the internal dynamo driving you to righteousness

As an inseparable branch of the Holy Trinity
The Holy Ghost in its Pentecostal duty
Fills us with the internal energy and enlightenment
To discover our inner peace, power, and enrichment

Let the wondrous winds of the Holy Spirit
Fill your flute to furnish flowing music
As you do the divine dance of independence
Aligned with small acts of spiritual significance

BRIEF HISTORY OF CHRISTIANITY

Christianity started in the first century in Judea
With a handful of faithful followers
Predominantly Jews in a small, private setting
Over a communal meal and worshipping

Women played a significant role.
As the practice and progress of Christianity unfold
Based on Jesus' life, teachings, and ministry
And His death and resurrection mystery

Through the hard work and devotion of disciples
Who traversed and preached in many countries
Christianity spread throughout the Roman Empire
Despite opposition and persecution from those in power

Challenged by the choice between Christ and Emperor worship
A significant sect secretly sailed on the Christian ship
Christianity became the official religion in time
Under the Great Emperor Constantine

Early Christianity was scarred by schism.
Different branches emerged with great enthusiasm.
Catholicism, Protestantism, and Orthodoxy
Spreading in Europe, Asia, Africa, and other countries

Renaissance, Reformation, and modernity
Brought a deluge of denominations to Christianity

Martin Luther's challenges to Catholic practices
Ushered in Anglicans, Lutherans, Pentecostals, and Calvinists

Along the Christian chronological corridor
The religion was under the radical and reformist radar
That covered and circumvented its power
Through the whims and fancies of Monarchs and Emperors

European Monarchs played a vital part.
In giving Christianity a significant start
Making it the official religion of the State
With solid support coming from the Papal plate

Subsequent papal reforms injected new policies.
Enforcing doctrinal decrees and clerical celibacy
And introducing the separation of Powers
Between the Church and the government structures

Christianity was checkered and corrupted by the Crusades
Resulting in the loss of countless deathly daze
And infected by the iniquity of the Inquisition
Thus, demoralizing and denigrating religion

Christianity was spread in Greek and Latin, written and oral
With emphasis on the four Gospels and Letters of Paul
As clergy and laity became more literate
It took on a liberal and lavish language gait

Christianity's ideology provided a pivotal pillar.
For new ways of thinking and cultural clamor

For spiritual substance, meaning, and morality
Which was conveniently provided by Christianity

Generally accepting baptism and communion.
Creeds, covenants, Commandments, and confessions
Mass attendance, Sabbath observance, and special holidays
Giving tithes, alms, prayerful service, and praise

As the world expanded widely and openly
Owing to scientific developments and discovery
Europe embarked on explosive colonization
Increasing imperialism and the export of religion

Wherever European colonial powers stretched
Christianity was practiced and preached
It was also taken into the Aboriginal reservations
To fill the flock of Christians

Colonialism exploited bodies within its hold
Christianity arrived to soften and save souls
Established States actively supported the Churches
To evangelize and enlighten the masses

Men in the missionary movement
Sailed out to a different continent
Setting up schools, churches, and Societies
To spread the creed of Christianity

Modern-day development adopts freedom of religion.
Freedom of thought, speech, and association

So, people are free to pursue the religion of their choice
With lofty liberalism to express their voice

In this liberal spirit and religious freedom
Christianity has penetrated every nation
Making it the largest religion with 3 billion followers
Representing 31 % of all the globe trotters

RELIGION ON THE ROUGH ROAD

The path of religion throughout the ages
Strewn with scripture and sacred images
Guiding a man through trials and tribulations
In his search for serenity and salvation
A path now plagued with a plethora of problems
Putting religion on a rough ride to mayhem
Challenged by science and technology
Degraded and denigrated by infernal ideology
Festered and fractured by doubts and depravity
Constricted by the growth of materialistic devotees
Belief in religion is severely shaken
By intellectuals who think they're already in heaven
The religious road is forsaken forever
By the majority who seek alternative pleasure
Following the mundane path to richness and relief
Bereft of a sacred system of belief
The righteous road to religion
It is riddled with attractive, tempting distractions
Deceiving and imprisoning believers
Victims of satanic enterprises and endeavors
The deadly dragnet of addiction
Steadily swallowing up souls in its suction
Drugs, alcohol, gambling, and other vices
Wheedle would-be believers in their clutches
Resulting in a decline in church attendance
And participation in religious observance

Folks foment fickle and frivolous excuses
Not to attend mass or service in sacred places
No time available for divine devotion
No money to buy new clothes to impress the congregation
Some don't like the priest's personality
Too gaudy, gay, graceless, or of low morality
Instead of focusing on the meaningful message
They prefer to indulge in collateral damage
When religion becomes more commercialized
And its practice is less spiritualized
It is opening the door to its own decadence
As the spirit is swamped by material abundance
Instead of Jesus being the reason for the season
Santa Claus commercial claptrap wins with reason
Edging out spirituality from religion
Throwing the world into a glamorous dungeon
Where materialism becomes the charming, credible creed
As people pursue the pleasures of the flesh with greed
Thus, churches slowly become musty museums
With relics of what was once holy and wholesome
Pews languish in the luxury of emptiness
Missing the warmth that generated spiritual liveliness
Hallowed objects and texts of Scripture
Overtaken by dust and tiny creatures
Driving nails into the coffin of religion
Sending God into eternal oblivion
It's time to wake up and smell the burning incense
Before your borrowed body bows in demise
Enter the energy emanating from cosmic Consciousness

That you can refer to as your God or Goddess
Remember that you sprung from that Source
And created with a pre-determined course
From the womb to the tomb
Living a life that's death-doomed
You came from nowhere to here
And you're going back from here to nowhere
You're a wavelength of spiritual energy
Vibrating on a frequency allowed by the Almighty
You're a mere transient extension rod
Of an omnipotent, omniscient, omnipresent God
Enjoying earthly life at His mercy
So, seek His blessings and glory
Through wholesome ways of worship and praise
In faith or religion, you were raised in
Remember that you came with nothing
And you will undoubtedly be leaving without anything
Why amassing money and material stuff
When your life will soon be snuffed
You were endowed with soul and spirit
That interacts with the Creator of it
Connect and call Him
In sincere prayers, meditation, and hymns
He responds by connecting to your conscience
By way of intuition and clairvoyance
No science or technology
Is capable of such a wondrous entity
So don't waste the present opportunity
To Align with the Supreme Divine Authority

Know ye that the essence of religion is peace and love
The basis from which good things are hove
The tenets and teachings of religion
If followed with devout passion
Leads to a good life, fulfilled and rewarding
Guided, guaranteed by the grace of God's blessings
A blessed life is devoid of corruption and conflict
Ungodly life is sinful and sick
Live in God's love, not Satan's power
God gives and saves, Satan takes and devours
Don't use religion as a weapon
Misguided by the sentiments of the Demon
To destroy lives through jihad or crusade
Value all lives that God has made
He hasn't created lives for you to kill
By your stupid, senseless, satanic skill
There is no room or reason in religion
To despise, denigrate, or destroy God's creation
Learn to accept and appreciate your fellow beings
Allow the power of love to grant good feelings
To overcome your bitterness, bias, and bigotry
Becoming an integral part of enlightened humanity
Priests in the hierarchy wield powers
Must dismount their high horses and ivory towers
And humbly walk and talk with one and all
Not just befriending the few in their prescribed hall
Immoral for priests or pastors to pander
To the rich, famous, or those in power
Fishing for favors to fatten their feathers

To fly higher than their Master
They must strive to emulate examples
Of their religion's Prophets and Disciples
Whether it's Jesus' simplicity and sanctity
Budha's sacrifice and serenity
Or Ram's rigors of righteousness
Or Mohammed's mercy and meekness
When priests become exemplary spiritual models
The instruments of religion yield and yodel
Producing the musical mantra of devotion
To receptive ears in the congregation
Religion thrives as the brotherly bond expands
Among clergy, laity, and the ordinary man
When we manifest love for one another
God above ceases to worry and wonder
This love is a religion in its own rights
Capable of making all things beautiful and bright
Parents need to be proud practitioners of their faith
Conversant with words flowing from God's own gate
Transmitting the religious principles and practices
To their children, friends, and relatives
A paramount goal of every nation
To give and promote freedom of religion
Keeping politics out of the religious domain
Must be the rule of the national game
Scholls and other institutions of learning
Must incorporate religious knowledge and teaching
Suffering the little, impressionable darlings
To grow in the grace of God's blessings

There is no substitute for religion
Created by man under God's inspiration
Given to us as a guide, a map, a compass
Travelling the days of our lives from first to last
Science and technology provide ease and comfort
But religion releases joy and self-worth.
That is deep down in every one of us
Made possible by a Divine so gracious
Strengthen your belief in the Creator
Whose infinite, invisible power
Can perform anything, even miracles
To prompt, protect, and provide for His peoples
Belief is the basic support of all religion
The stronger the belief, the deeper the devotion
All God requires on your part
Are a pure mind and a clean heart
No expensive or glamorous garment
No ostentatious order of material appeasement
No earthly icons or idols to worship
No golden or magnificent building for praise and fellowship
Just satisfy the spiritual yearning
To connect with God, the Father everlasting
Obtaining enlightenment and self-actualization
Eternal bliss, nirvana, and salvation

THE ABC OF GOD (Wonderful Words)

GOD is..........
Almighty, absolute, and awesome
Benevolent, blessed, and beautiful
Caring, compassionate, and comforting
Divine, devout, and devoted
Eternal, ennobled, and esteemed
Forgiving, faithful, and faultless
Gracious, great, and generous
Holy, honorable, and humane
Infinite, idolized, and immaculate
Joyful, just, and jealous
Kind, Kingly, and knowledgeable
Loving, laudable, and lenient
Merciful, magnanimous, and majestic
Noble, nurturing, and noted
Omnipotent, omnipresent, and omniscient
Perfect, pure, and praiseworthy
Quick, qualified, and quiet
Righteous, reliable, and revered
Sovereign, sanctimonious, and sincere
Trustworthy, tender, and true
Upright, unblemished, and uplifting
Virtuous, venerable, and victorious

Wonderful, worshipful, and wise
X-elect, X- alter, and X- luted
Yes, yours and yielding

Zealous, zone-free, and zooming

ADVANTAGES AND DISADVANTAGES OF FOLLOWING JESUS

1. **LOVE:** You learn the lessons of Love, enjoying the magic, mystery, and beauty of love by sharing it selflessly and unconditionally. On the other hand, when you fail to cultivate love, you become vain and bitter by withholding it selfishly.

2. **HUMILITY:** You honor and hold on to Humility. You do not boss people around or bully them. You come to respect modesty and subservience and sit lowly with dignity. On the contrary, by refusing to be humble, you bully and belittle others and force yourself upward through corrupt, unethical means.

3. **TRUTH:** You trust, typify, and train in Truth. When you are tender, trade, and talk in truth, you become free, uncorrupted, and pure. Thy truth shall set Thee free. On the contrary, when you avoid truth and deal in doubts, deception, and delusion, you end up feeling miserable, mean, and mortified.

4. **PEACE:** You practice, preach, perch, and play in Peace. Instead of pulling punches, triggers, and knives, you turn the other cheek. Letting go and walking away from the source of trouble keeps conflict, fight, and war at bay. Conversely, when you do not allow the power of Peace to prevail, you open the floodgates to unease, violence, turbulence, armed conflict, and even homicide. Tooth for a tooth triggers toothlessness.

5. **SIMPLICITY:** You savor, solemnize, and stand for Simplicity. You seek and settle for simple things, nothing flamboyant, sophisticated, cumbersome, and complicated that cost an arm and a leg. On the other hand, when you work your butt off and borrow money to have the best car, house, clothes, and menus to impress people who couldn't care less. And having no time to enjoy the simple, natural, free things Mother Nature offers.

6. **GRATITUDE:** You gravitate and gracefully grow in the grandeur of Gratitude. Always giving thanks for the gifts and blessings of life not only opens barns of blissful abundance and assurance but also releases unspeakable inner joy that is divinely aligned to your being. On the contrary, failure to give thanks for all the good things that come to you only shuts the door to the greater flow of such blessings. Not showing gratitude breeds selfishness, an inflated ego, and greed, which impede the release of the great joy inherent in body and soul.

7. **CHARITY:** You cultivate and cherish the cheerfulness, civility, and complacency crafted in Charity. Giving alms and donations to worthy causes not only pleases God, the Giver of everything, but it unleashes the freedom and beauty of your soul and entire being. Giving generously helps secure a large grant. In contrast, reluctance and failure to give alms and worthwhile donations to any cause stifles the freedom and sweetness of the soul. Selfishness and greed block the bounty and beauty of the Universe's blessings.

8. **PURITY:** You prioritize, portray, price, and pursue Purity. Cleanliness is next to Godliness. Being pure in heart, body, and mind qualifies you to be a sinless child of God. You value decency, selflessness, honesty,

justice, and compassion. Conversely, having impure, unclean thoughts, words, and deeds delivers you into the dungeon of defilement, depravity, disaster, and destruction: you court corruption, greed, envy, jealousy, and the whole nine yards of immorality.

9. **FORGIVENESS:** You fathom and flourish on the felicity of Forgiveness. Forgiving others for wrongs done to you can bring cardiovascular relief and lift psychological burden. You consciously shut the door to retaliation and open new ones to refreshing, recharged, and rejuvenated releases. In contrast, when you fail to forgive folks for hurting or harming you, you ramp up the road to revenge and retaliation. This will only lead to friction, fights, frustration, and felony. A heart full of stones can only shatter the glass of glory

MAKE JESUS YOUR PROTECTOR

Inculcate and hold tight to the following pieces of advice.

1. Have firm faith and belief in Jesus, God in the flesh. You can do or achieve anything through Christ, who strengthens you.

2. Accept Jesus as your Shield, the righteous rock to rely on.

3. Follow His examples to be peaceful, loving, and helpful.

4. Embrace and engross in His teachings and principles.

5. In despair or depression, "Let not your heart be troubled ". Be strong and positive. Take Your problems to the Lord.

6. Remember that Jesus never reacted violently to any circumstance. Refuse to respond in haste or anger to what is thrown at you. Use the small space between stimulus and response to choose safe, healthy ways to respond.

7. When in difficulty or danger, stop and think what Jesus would do in such a situation. Focusing faithfully on Christ will fortify you.

8. Becoming chaste and sinless like Jesus gives you a clean and credible character. Having no skeleton in your closet makes you saintlike, unstoppable, and unshakeable.

9. Although Jesus knew about His impending death, He was not worried. Boldly, he faced current events and realities. Never be anxious about the future or the past. Confine yourself to the present, which you can control. Worrying about future apprehensions or past mistakes only robs you of valuable time to make the most of the moments at hand.

10. Heed the warning of Jesus to be wary of wolves in sheep's clothing. Be wise; be mindful and aware of everything and everyone around you. You invite trouble when you drop your guard.

11. Like Jesus, learn to trade fear for faith; violence for virtue; loathing for love; bitterness for better; deceit for decency; corruption with compassion; sayer for Sower; greed for gratitude; fretting for forgiveness; trickery with truth; inertia with industry; negativity with positivity.

12. Be empowered by the Eucharist (Holy Communion) and be washed in the blood of Jesus.

13. Keep company with true and active Christians. This will support and solidify spiritual soundness and security.

14. Be anchored in the unfailing peace and love of Christ. A peace and love that surpasses all understanding. No weapon formed against you shall prosper.

CHRISTMAS IN CHRISTIANITY

Christmas centers on the birth of Jesus Christ
The advent of the Savior during a moral crisis
Today, Christmas itself is in crisis and chaos
Requiring a second coming of Christ Jesus

Christmas is filled with festivity and felicity
It's the most celebratory and ceremonial entity
Of Christianity and its global observance
Having the most attention and significance

Practically everyone knows what Christmas is
Happily joining in its celebration without fuss
Consumed in its character and commercialism
Heralding happy holidays in the high season

Jesus is the main reason for the season
Has diminished drastically to the point of treason
Giving way to the seductive charm of commercialism
At the expense of Nativity, spiritual idealism

People shop robustly with religious intensity.
In a spirit of good cheer and alacrity
Buying goodies and the conveniences of comfort
Frantically and sparing no effort

Commercialism causes people to recalibrate, renew.
Out with the old, and in with the new

Savings and the wallets take a liberal licking
Furnishing, feasting, toys, and gift-giving

Folks across all faiths revel in the Christmas tree
A festive centerpiece displayed ostentatiously
In homes, offices, public places, beautiful and bright
The evergreen representation of life and Light

The Christmas tree has a pagan origin
But later adapted and Christianized by Pilgrims
Representing Jesus as the Tree of Life and living
He is the vine and we the branches abiding

Much time, enthusiasm, energy, and money
It is devoted to the presence of a Christmas tree
With decorative lights, trinkets, and the Star of Bethlehem
Positioned at the top and pointing towards Heaven

The neatly packaged presents at the tree's bottom
Represent the good fruits we cultivate and count on
It's a mark of generosity, goodwill, and favors
Shared by family, friends, and neighbors

People bake black cake, pound cake, and fruit cake
Prepare festive meals, enriching and elaborate
Wash it down with a leaded and flavored drink
To celebrate Christmas with a restrained religious link

Fewer faithful followers of Jesus
Attend midnight Mass to welcome Christmas

Praying, singing carols, and hailing Mother Mary
In a traditional manner, to observe His birth anniversary

They embrace Jesus as the reason for the season
Others see shopping, festivity, and feasting as the reason
The true meaning lies in the act of Incarnation
God taking human form for the Nativity celebration

Christmas symbolizes God's love for us.
And the peace, goodwill, and eternal life given by Jesus
The real reasons we must appreciate and accept
As the foundation of Christian belief and concept

Christianity is on a collision course.
Challenged and cheapened by commercial force
Necessitating the urgency to create a beautiful balance
Between commercialism and Christmas observance

The Nativity must be religiously revered and honored
Christmas must be basically Jesus-centered
The church must emphasize and invigorate its spirituality
To match or minimize commercial supremacy

Individuals must reinforce their religious responsibility.
Waxed in the word and ways of the Lord with piety
Practicing and promoting the virtues of Christianity
To sustain sanity, security, success, and sanctity of humanity

Failure to fan the fervent fire of religion
Refusal to be guided by sacred education

Will undermine a sound cultural foundation
And ultimately lead to self-destruction

Render to Jesus what is Jesus'
Restore the spirituality of Christmas
Embrace the true meaning of Nativity
Let it be the blessed beginning of life's journey

THE LESSONS OF LOVE

Jesus made constant reference to the power of love
That follows and flows from the divine Source above
A love that exhibits mysterious power
So captivating, calm, and clever
Endowed with excitable, endearing emotion
To exude exquisite, graceful elevation
Imbued with utmost, utter compassion
That transforms life into every generation
Dissolving, dispelling detestation
Empowering people in all nations
Loves is loaded with the antidote for animosity
And the energy to erode enmity
Turning trials and tragedy
Into comfort and comedy
It's more potent than education
In eradicating deadly discrimination
Based on color, creed, caste, and condition
Love is like energy in matter
Constantly changing forms and features
Manifesting itself in myriad ways
Like a rainbow on rainy days
Love is a living, lasting spirit in eternity
Equivalent in essence to the Almighty
It's the expression of God's glory
The foundation of all Faiths and fraternity
Love is the winsome, welcome wind sublime

Transcending territories and time
Blowing blithely and blissfully with grace
Impacting and influencing every soul it embraces
Whether it's sentimental, sacred, or sexual
Love consumes us overall
With exceptional, extraordinary ecstasy
An enduring, bountiful beauty
When everything fails
Love certainly prevails
Love is invisible money
Can be earned, can be given earnestly
Can be spent but not burned
Because it is always going around
It's the best, benign investment
The more one puts out, indeed
The greater the returns, indeed
Interest grows as deposits increase
Capital climbs as withdrawals decrease
The miser can hide or hoard it brave
But I cannot take it to the grave
Love shared is love multiplied
Becomes useless currency when withheld
Love reserved is an uncashed cheque
Cash it and spread it without an object
Give it generously: reap bountifully
Shower, scatter, and spend lavishly
Why depart this earth in haste or hate?
Lingering longer in love that lifts and elates

THE ESSENTIALS OF FORGIVENESS

Jesus emphasized the virtue of forgiveness.
Of which He was the greatest
With a classic demonstration on the cross at Calvary
Asking God to forgive man and his iniquity
Forgiveness is the act of pardoning
People for their sins and wrongdoing
It is a virtue born out of bravery
Absolving the offender, appeasing the offended
Love is the mystery of forgiveness
Bringing relief and redress
Forgiveness clears the conscience
And ushers in deliverance
Be quick to forgive
Try not to be vindictive
Forgive those who bring hurt or stain
But do not forget their name
Cause you don't want them to do the same
For you to forgive again
The arrow that caused the emotional hurt
You boldly pull out with great effort
Instead of redirecting it to your enemy
You break and bury openly
To placate and humble them
Taking away their ship, sail, and helm
Forgiveness opens the door to a renewed relationship
But vengeance fragments fellowship

Forgiveness has the connecting power
Which brings estranged people together
It can surely open the window to heaven
Forgiving wrongdoers seventy times seven
Forgiveness is the creator of concessions
Between violently rivaling nations
Willing to bury the hatchet
Will provide mutual benefit
If you happen to inflict pain or distress
Be quick to seek forgiveness
The whims and weaknesses of human nature
Make wrongdoing a prevalent feature
Which can be easily resolved
By those willing to absolve
If you don't want to forgive
Just don't create any form of mischief
If due forgiveness is not forthcoming
Don't go hunting or begging
Humbly assumed it was granted
And the discomfort will be dissipated
Having to accept your fault and say sorry
Is humanity's number one worry
Consumed by pride and vanity
Stubbornly refuses to seek amenity
Forgiveness secures succor for the soul
Releasing restoration to mind and body bold
Forgiveness subsides the sand in the storm
Opening a new vista for life to go on
To receive any form of forgiveness

One must first confess
The wrong or sin one commits
For the forgiver to forget it
Many conceive confession as condemnatory
Expecting criticism, damning, and desultory
Confession demands humble condescension
Completing the act of contrition
Honestly delivered with forthright courage
Gives confession its consummate leverage
Forgiveness is a two-way street
Where forgiver and sinner meet
Morally making the exulting exchange
Riding along the restoration range
Refusal or reluctance to forgive
Will not bring about reprieve
It will only worsen conditions
Winding the world to woeful damnation
The more you forgive
The more the Lord will concede

THE NICENE CREED

Creeds support and sustain standard Christian belief
They become the beacon and buttress of belief
Capturing the essence of the religion
Guiding believers in their worship and devotion

Creeds refer to the universality of the Church
And not a specific denomination or ideological perch
Creeds are central to common grounds
On which religion arises and abounds

At the very beginning of Christianity
Believers were forced into seclusion and secrecy
Theology was tinged and tarnished by disputes
Troubled by teething problems to repute

Spiritual matters came to a head, bold and bright
When Constantine gave Christianity the green light
Church councils met in the city of Nicaea
And finally arrived at a panacea

The convention came up with the Nicene Creed
Which represented the spiritual Seed
From which universal Christianity grew
Into a gigantic global Tree, tried and true

THE APOSTLES' CREED

The Apostles' Creed is widely recognized and accepted
As the oldest symbol of faith that the Apostles perfected
A sublime summary of Christian belief
Bringing much liturgical and religious relief

The Creed captures the central crux of Christianity
Presenting precious pieces of piety
Belief in God, the Creator, and Jesus Christ, the Son
His life, death, resurrection, and return

GIVING

A critical component of Jesus' preaching
Had to do with the act and duty of giving
Giving is love in action
Born out of care and consideration
Expressed towards people with low incomes and in poverty
Or causes and cases that are worthy
Giving is grounded in generosity
It's a manifestation of mercy
It is more blessed to donate
Than to extend your collection plate
Giving contains a mystery hidden
Bringing back more than what is given
No one knows that secret
Except the Master who blesses it
Giving one's time, talent, and treasure
Creates an emotional height and rapture
Pleasant and soothing to the soul
A salubrious sentiment to have and hold
Those who give freely
Have less burden to carry
Giving with the expectation of return
Cancels out the blessings there on
Giving from your extra or abundance
It is of little or no significance
Donating your last penny or shilling
It is a sacrifice that merits the highest blessing

Good to give what you get
Not what you don't have yet
The best gift from Jesus is unconditional love
Like the love we receive from above
Or the kind Mother Theresa did offer
To the homeless, unfortunate souls in Calcutta
Genuine love given under any condition
It is a good gift in the human equation
Donating money and material things
To alleviate human suffering
It is a commendable act of benevolence
With exemplary altruistic influence
If you want more, then give more
To needful beggars at your door
Activate your heart of charity
Join the humanitarian host of humanity
Let your positive, tender feeling
Underscores your acts of giving
Done in simple, sweet, secret ways
Not as manifestations of public display
Gifts given to strangers
More blessed than gifts to family members
Gifts to family members obligate them in a way
To return the favors someday
Giving presents on special days and weddings
Represents a cultural, mutual dealing
With no basis for blessings
Or expression of charitable feelings
Giving gifts to people in need and strangers

Who has no scope of returning the favors
Brings abundant blessings to donors
And high marks in the eyes of the Holy Father
The great giver, in return, expects nothing
For his generous gesture of giving
Not even expressed sentiments of gratitude
Or the recognition of his benevolent attitude
The wise one gives away everything
That he accumulates whilst living
Cause he knows he came with nothing
And he's going back without anything
The gracious acts of loving and giving
Only happens while you are living
So don't live and act miserly
With a humble heart, give freely
Give and spend liberally
And the good Lord will reward bountifully

THE LAW DIVINITY

Jesus is the human display of Divinity
An icon of Incarnation worshipped by humanity
A lasting leg of the law of Divinity
That pervades piously over cosmic reality

There's overwhelming trust in the law of Gravity
And fervent faith in the wonders of electricity
But shallow belief in the law of Divinity
Which embraces the power of the Holy Trinity

Invisible, infinite power flows in Divinity
Like the unseen current in electricity
Divinity covers and controls Cosmic dynamics
Like the physical laws of Physics

Humanity hinges on the hegemony of Divinity
Soulfully breathing it like oxygen of eternity
To live righteously, spiritually each day
Despite the noise and friction in the fray

We are all waves in the ocean of Divinity
Rising, rolling, rocking on the shores of humanity
But anchored, activated by the depth of Divinity
The supernatural succour of peace and serenity

Jesus constantly referred to the Divine power
Emanating eternally from the merciful Father

The Creator and Designer of all deeds
And every word which from His mouth proceeds

We're challenged and colored by clouds of chaos
But can rely on the sky of Divinity to save us
Just seeking and praying for divine deliverance
Timely, slow but eventually arriving in full assurance

The Trinitarian principle of the law of Divinity
Is generated and governed by the Almighty
Invoking the presence of human deities
Or the dynamism of the Holy Spirit activities

Laws of Nature can be observed and absorbed
But the law of Divinity is spiritually internalized
Not by the senses but the soul in symphony
Dancing to the spiritual tune of Divinity

The law of Divinity operates in peace and calmness
As soul seeks connection with the hands of Holiness
The divine law is not governed by natural force
But through the Father, Son and Holy Ghost

Meditate in silent, serene moment
Be covered by your spiritual garment
Let your soul wonder to wondrous height
Unblemished by any forms of secular flight

The law of Divinity works best
When you don't put it to a test

Just relax and watch the process unfold
And touches your sweet soul

Ever experience any wonderful windfall or benediction
That defies explanation or comprehension
It's a manifestation of the law of Divinity
A divine deposit made by the mission of mercy

The law of Divinity follows no structure or pattern
For mankind to fathom or understand
It doesn't emanate from an adhoc assembly
But follows faithfully the dictates of the Almighty

An omnipotent, omnipresent and omniscient power
That knows every earthly encounter
And intervenes at the right moment
To bring solution to problems and predicament

Laws of the land employ disciplined forces
To effect adherence and compliance by natives
The law of Divinity deploys angels and the Holy Spirit
To bring about remedy, relief and resolute benefit

Divinity adopts various forms, features and fashion
And uses means, methods, mechanism and motions
To carry out positive and miraculous transformation
In sync and alignment with karma and devotion

When anything good beyond belief
Happens to usher in remarkable relief

That's the law of Divinity in action
In its immutable, interminable manifestation

In His life, teachings and ministry
Jesus functioned within the law of Divinity
As a secular symbol of its representation
And a testimony of its revelation

We perceive the signs and symptoms of Gravity
And experience its pull and magnetic potency
Similarly we note the ways and wonders of Divinity
And enjoy its blessings and mercy

DEALING WITH A DIVINE DILEMMA

Currently, Christianity is at a crossroad.
Where faith and following implode
Caught between spiritual and devilish forces
Man is challenged to choose the right course

The constant clash between evil and goodness
And the rift and ravage of righteousness
Exacerbated by the power of God against Satan
Expose the dilemma of longevity versus oblivion

God sees man swimming and sinking in sin
That requires Jesus' second coming
Not only to save us from sinful degradation
But to save the world from annihilation

Christianity today faces great and growing difficulty
To uphold and affirm genuine loyalty
To the only begotten Son, Jesus Christ
As the saving Lord, who paid the ultimate price

They prioritize other magnets over the Master
Money and materialism provide short-lived succour
With little or no time to worship
Jesus Christ in His eternal, divine Lordship

Many Christians go to church regularly.
Following the conventional path, right and holy
Finding difficulty, the real Jesus to find
Because of mundane thoughts and a wandering mind

Going in a charming carriage, fully festooned
Like an empty, embellished balloon
Admirable but devoid of spiritual prowess
To have a deep, genuine relationship with Jesus

They cherish the crucifix, love the liturgy
But it lacks the full focus on Jesus' divinity
It's not easy to love the Lord unconditionally
With all your soul, mind, and body

Firm faith and belief in Jesus Christ
Is compromised by distractions and digital devices
Science, technology, and artificial intelligence
Are we cheating Christianity of its significance and substance

Prayers have become empty words in the wind
When trust in the Lord recedes and rescinds
Half-hearted and ostentatious religious practice
Only drive Jesus towards the precarious precipice

Congregational characters are captivated by the clergy's charisma
Rather than by the essentials of Jesus as their spiritual Leader
A significant section sees the church as a social outing
And less to do with serious, sincere worshipping

Thrust the tendency of priests and pastors
Placing priority on the persona of the messengers
Focus instead on the quality of the message
Based on Christian essentials and scriptural passages

How many put the message over the messenger
How many place preferences of the priest over the Savior
How many focus on God rather than the members of the congregation
How many make mundane desires spoil salvation

Is church-going a welcome break from daily routine
Is it gratification to gyrate in gaudy clothing
Or an auspicious occasion to meet and socialize
Or is it an opportunity to worship Jesus as your personal prize?

Analysts and critics can bear witness.
To the fact that religion is big business
Organised and orchestrated via commercial management
Mega-collection, fundraising, and audio-video sales engagement

Love of money and money-mindedness
Will drive Christianity into the wilderness
Moreover, the majority worship the Almighty Dollar
Rather than praying for a supper

Fractured faith and broken belief
Resulting from financial relief
Is shaking the foundation of Christianity
Requiring divine intervention to restore its integrity

Facing the current widespread dilemma
Church and State must work together
Providing recourse, resource, and resolution
To resuscitate Christianity and secure salvation

Church buildings must be measured by membership
To avoid financial and maintenance hardship
Emphasis must be on people and the gospel
Not on the physical attractions of the chapel

Church must adapt to the demands of demographics
Concentrate on crowds and outreach logistics
Manage methods of ministry to appeal to all ages
Let the liturgy of Love give the mission mileage

Mankind needs to realign itself urgently.
With Jesus Christ and the Holy Trinity
Develop a sincere personal relationship with Him
The Prince of Peace and King of Kings

Stop pretending and playing a pious Christian.
Loud, empty words of worship are a disdain
Sincerely, secretly, and steadfastly stay with Jesus
Walk with Him, talk with Him, remain in His compass

Concentrate on the countenance of Christ.
Acknowledge and appreciate this symbol of sacrifice
Focus on the face of forgiveness, peace, and love
And the blessings He can send down from above

Stop putting your trust in the arms of flesh
Seek Jesus for body, mind, and soul redress
Man, money, and machine will one day fail
But the power and compassion of Jesus always prevail

Truly trust in the healing power of Jesus
Earnestly embrace His teachings so precious
Open your heart and willingly accept Him
With his strength, you can achieve anything

FINAL THOUGHTS

As the major religion in the global confluence
Christianity has grown in presence and influence
Touching hearts and souls in every corner
With faithful, far-reaching, and fervent fervour

Blessedly built on sanctity and divinity.
Stemming strong from the Holy Trinity
The grace of God, the Son, and the Holy Spirit
The consecrated components are worthy of worship

Christianity provides the benign brightness.
To navigate through spiritual darkness
The Light and Love of Life: A Peaceful Expedition
And an injunction and inspiration towards salvation

Christ is the central personification of Christianity
His Advent, life, teachings, and ministry
His suffering, trials, tribulations, and crucifixion
Culminated in His holy resurrection

With a history of hindrances, disputes, and divisions
Theological turbulence and riotous ramifications
Crusades, the Inquisition, and socio-political opposition
Christianity survived and succeeded with distinction

State and Church cooperate eventually.
To let Christianity flow and flourish freely
Religious institutions are established universally
To promote its value, virtues, and validity

Following doctrines from Ecclesia, Synods, and Papacy
Executed by an ordained clerical hierarchy
In expanding sects and different denominations
Exercising their spiritual freedom and devotion

Devotion and faithfulness fluctuated over time.
Churches are getting emptier as attendance declines
Old faithfuls die, not fully replaced by the young
Distracted by modernity and its magnum

Christianity is witnessing a seismic spiritual shift
From Jesus and the Gospel to personalized lift
Where the elements of ego and selfishness
Override the essentials of righteousness

Digital distraction and artificial intelligence
It is gradually corroding Christianity's influence
The search for secular satisfaction
It is steadfastly shaking Christianity's foundation

Christianity remains a significant spiritual path.
Based on principles that Jesus did impart
Followed faithfully, it offers a rewarding life
Filled with the power of love and peace over strife

Reduced and stripped to its core
Christianity is the epitome of love for sure
God's love; love of God and love of yours truly
Love of neighbor, friends, foes, and family

Love is the embodiment of Jesus' two commandments
Love of God and love of neighbor sentiments
Remains the broad base of Christianity
The energy and engine of its longevity

Like other religions, Christianity is all about love
Raw, refined, recycled, replete, and renewed love
The hallowed hallmark of humanity
The overpowering archangels of Christianity

This omnipotent, omnipresent, and omniscient love
Constitutes a religion around and above
Denominations, sects, institutions, and social structures
Mustering and moving skeptics, atheists, critics, and believers

The dynamics and power of this love
Connects and consumes everyone in the global glove
It becomes a religion without a name
No fanfare, no finance, fancy, nor fame

In this love, people with low incomes find happiness
The downtrodden and marginalized get gladness
For all, it is the springboard for salvation
The beauty, bliss, and glory of civilization

Guided by the power of this love candle
The rich camel can go through the eye of a needle
Guided and governed by its everlasting light
Channelling charity and compassion left and right

This infinite, infectious love and its power
Needs no sophisticated, elaborate physical structure
No special liturgy or ecclesiastical embellishment
Just a pure heart and moral entrenchment

This is the kind of love Jesus preached
A lasting love that Christianity does teach
The all-curing love that man desperately needs
Bringing the blessings, it flourishes and feeds

When in despair and despondency
Invoke and activate this love's potency
Which resides deep down in your body
Capable of miracles and remarkable remedy

God's love for human beings
Sent Jesus to endure great sufferings
And it was Jesus' love for us
That He willingly died on the cross

No one knows the time or hour
When He'll return in shining splendour
To repeat that fateful favour
As the masterly Messiah and sanctified Savior

Civilization will collapse the world over.
But my words will remain forever.
Live by the word of God.
In peace, love, and dignity unflawed

GRATITUDE

Jesus expounded and extolled the virtue of gratitude
The act of blessing, which results in plenitude
From the Source of Creation and distribution
Of all good things to the souls of supplication

Jesus took the five loaves and two fish
Lift them and give thanks for a limited dish
Miraculously, they multiply in magnitude
By the mysterious blessings of gratitude

The more gratitude is shown or expressed
More rewards and returns become manifest
Gratitude reserved, restrained, or retracted
Make blessings, beauty, and bliss blighted

Gratitude is more than the thanks expressed
For who or what you are and what you possess
It's the phenomenal pipeline that perpetuates a plethora
Of beauty, blessings, balance, and euphoria

Gratitude expressed steadily and sincerely.
For deeds and things of goodness and beauty
Opens the door to satisfaction and contentment
The basis of health, happiness, and appeasement

Showing gratitude for things in your possession
Fosters the feelings of fullness and fruition

That dispels the desire for more
To come to you or land on your shore

Give gratitude for the gift of life
Being a male or a female, husband or wife
Living in a beautiful universe
Delving into delights, deep and diverse

Give Mother Nature the deserved gratitude.
For all consumables provided in plenitude
For the invisible energy that ensures the cycles
Of returns and recurrences in blessed principles

Saying thank you to the sun for its eternal energy
That gives us warmth, light, and the prodigy
This underscores the universal laws of occurrence
That guarantees its continual presence and substance

Be grateful for the bud that blooms and flowers
Providing beauty and joy forever
Assuring awesomeness and aesthetic inspiration
In the face of failure and frustration

Be grateful for parents who brought you here
With lasting love and costly care
So that your days on earth will be long
And joyful family experiences and memories prolong

Be grateful for your sophisticated body.
An integral part of the mysterious cosmology

Vibrating in its frequency of eternal energy
With the awesome assurance of being somebody

Be thankful for family, friends, and fraternity
Providing uplifting support and camaraderie
Towards maturity and the mastery of life's art
Premised and prompted by a grateful heart

Gratitude shown for kind words and actions
Invigorates and intensifies the law of attraction
As gratitude grows greater and more graceful
Blessings become bigger and bountiful.

Be thankful for your job, occupation, or profession
That provides the means to bring in the bacon
And gives the latitude to relate well with colleagues
And fades away frailty, frustration, and fatigues

Seniors, be grateful for the blessings of retirement
Thankful to God and employers for such an achievement
So that it lasts the longest while
Becoming the second child with a steady smile

Forever be grateful for life lived on earth
Keeping the faith, running your race from birth
With its ups and downs, best and bends
That one day comes to an end.

Faithfully follow Jesus' grateful gestures
Giving thanks for what lands on your shoulder

It is a good and gracious thing
Always to give God thanks for His blessing

BECOMING A BETTER AND BLESSED PERSON

Jesus opened the way and taught us the principles
To become better and blessed people
Walking and working under God's commandments
Living a life of lovliness and contentment

In a world flawed with friction and fight
There's a dire need to prohibit this plight
By becoming better members of society
Creating a world of seemliness and serenity

What a beautiful world it would be for all
Becoming better, brighter, and balanced individuals
Shunning selfishness, spite, and scorn
Embracing mutual respect, love, care, and concern

Personal prejudice, indifference, and intolerance
Cause detestable division and social distance
Breeding grounds for dismay and disunity
Inimical and injurious to peace and prosperity

Becoming a better person in society
One must master the means and measures of morality
Inculcating a lifestyle founded on humility and honesty
With a positive mindset for decency and dignity

A devilish disposition and questionable character
A recipe for ruinous conduct and disaster
Detrimental to self-worth and self-improvement
Unworthy of admiration and social development

Spare a word or two with your neighbor
Give compliments for appearances and good behavior
Vanishing vice and vibrating virtue
By opening delicate doors and accommodating avenues

Be a paragon of peace and patience
Learn to listen and savor silence
Setting exemplary attributes of a worthy role model
To mould minds, willing and able

Cultivate a sense of humor.
Joking and laughing with each other
Activating the antidote to an adversarial relationship
And actualizing an atmosphere of friendship

Never find faults in people.
Give suggestions to improve, simple, and gentle
No person parades on a platform of perfection
We all have defects and remissions

Get yourself a good, sound education.
To land a lucrative, likeable profession
Providing the wherewithal to support and sustain life
With minimum struggle, stress, and strife

Follow the example of Jesus for the longest while
By wearing a simple, steady smile
It enlightens and elevates your spirit
And sends a positive message to those seeing it

Heartily hang on to healthy habits.
Capable of catapulting you to the summit
Supported by a balanced diet, regular exercise
The secret to delaying demise

Learn to love yourself dearly.
Bless and adore every part of your body
Accept and appreciate what and who you are
Mindfully content with what you've got so far

With dedication and time to spare
Willingly, cheerfully become a valued volunteer
Offering salutary service to society with vigor
The hand of service is better than a word of prayer

Dress appropriately in clean clothes for a good reason
Attending special occasions in different seasons
Manifesting mature taste and sensibility
And poise, presence, and pride of probity

Encountering situations and folks in difficulty
Be quick to empathize and offer sympathy
Demonstrating concern, compassion, and care
To alleviate suffering and uplift those in despair

With goals in mind and purpose-oriented
Go forward, upward, and onward undaunted
In sincerity, simplicity, and humility
Bent on leaving a lasting legacy

Daily practice positive self-affirmation
I'm the best; I'm unstoppable; I'm a sensation
Don't rely on external support and surety
Count on self-validation and adequacy

Dig into and discover your inner strength
Earnestly explore and exploit to the fullest extent
Align and harness thoughts, emotions, and imagination
To bring about an extraordinary transformation

Appreciate an attitude of gratitude.
Credit the Creator for blessings in amplitude
Relish the right to be a child of the universe
A signature success; a delight deep and diverse.

OVERCOMING TEMPTATIONS

Be inspired by Jesus' triumph over temptation
Cultivate the will and strong determination
To fearlessly face the flirtations of the Devil
And ward off the consequences of evil
The Devil may be the orchestrator of every temptation
But it requires human nature for their perpetuation
Temptations never operate in a vacuum
They flex their muscles between womb and tomb.'
Once there is life
Temptation becomes the tool of strife
All temptations must first enter the mind
Then a willing, obedient body to find
To carry out the devious, devilish deeds
Which destroys us like a deadly disease
The mind is the mediator and manipulator
Between temptation and its operator
Temptation only becomes a successful operation
If the conscious mind gives permission
When the mind is disciplined and controlled
Temptations grow weak and cold
Satan, through the medium of the serpent
Played on Eve's mind to gain consent
For her to eat the forbidden fruit
Thus giving sin its original root
Satan has no axe to grind
In the presence of a perfect, positive mind

A classic case in point
Occurred in the wilderness joint
As he valiantly tried and failed three times
Getting Jesus to succumb to his deceiving designs
Minds must first be conscious
Of temptations in front of us
Deliberating and considering consequences
Will open up avenues of submission or defences
Ultimately, the mind makes the choice
Whether to regret or to rejoice
Letting down our God's guard
Opens the door to the Devil's vanguard
Satan has a way of approaching egos first
Before he caresses our conscience with a curse
Getting our bodies to submit to his evil devices
Doing sinful things against our wishes
With a clear conscience and God on our side
The Devil falters, flowing against the tide
So, the first form of temptation attack
Is to have righteousness intact
Following the word and laws of God
Makes the Devil mad and you glad
Cultivate and train the mind to use things
Not to love them as supreme Beings
The love of money is the incubator of temptations
Hatching a huge conspiracy of corruption
From graft and greed to perjury and prostitution
Scam and stealing to arson and assassination

To avoid the guile and grip of money
Just use wisely what you earn honestly
Money is not the Provider of everything
It cannot buy happiness and true blessings
When the temptation to steal prevails
Think of what getting caught entails
The shame, the ridicule, the prison internment
And let that be a damper and deterrent
Men moved by the temptation of sexual plunder
Must think of their victim as a sister or daughter
Women who are tempted to seduce a youngster
Must view their prey as a son or brother
Reason and emotion must be in positive gear
To slap temptation and scare
The emotions of sympathy and compassion
Can influence reason to overpower temptation
When reasoning and feelings are in the negative
Temptations are fed with explosives
People submit to the temptation to tell lies
To cover up imperfections, guiles, and wiles
Using lies as scapegoats and excuses
To defend deceit, dishonesty, and abuses
Millions are tempted to engage in acts of adultery
And have fallen victim to infidelity.
Clandestinely pursuing honey in sweet-hearting
With heart aches, divorce in the awakening
Thoughts of envy and jealousy
Have pushed people's lives into jeopardy

Having coveted their neighbor's personal property
Committing desperate deeds, causing misery
If you can't have what they possess
Be content with what's at your address
Resolutely resist the temptation to compare
To vanquish vanity and despair
The temptation to kill or murder
It's worse than the rest put together
Today, homicide is a daily drill
Cause folks fail to overcome the temptation to kill
Motivated by money, mischief, and reparation
They kill their way to senseless satisfaction
Why bloody your hands with murder
When can you be your brother's keeper?
Temptations are the torturous tests of times
Ever-present in all cultures and climes
As part of human nature
They test our willpower to overcome or surrender
If we overcome, then we succeed and stand tall
If we surrender or succumb, we fail and fall

JOKES ABOUT JESUS

THEOLOGICAL TITLES

Three boys were under a shady tree, boasting about their uncles.

First one said: "My uncle is a priest at Christ the King church. When people see him

They say "Reverend Father. "

The second said: "My uncle is the Bishop at Christ the Redeemer chapel. When people See him, they say, "Your Highness."

The third said: "That ain't nothing. My uncle is 7 feet tall, and he weighs 600 pounds

When he walks the street, people say, "Jesus Christ. "

Moral: When wits of reverence meet, holy sparks fly out.

A certain man had a faithful pet dog for 15 years. The dog died and he wanted to give his best friend a decent funeral. So he approached an Anglican priest in town.

"Father, can I have a proper funeral for my dog that died?

Priest said " we don't do funeral services for animals. But you can go to the country side and ask one of the Jumper Church people to do it. I am sure that they will do it. "

As the gentleman was leaving, he turned around and asked the Reverend.

"Father if I give them 5000 dollars do you think that they will do it.

Quickly the priest exclaimed "Why you didn't tell me that the dog was Christian???

Moral: Money makes the social and spiritual world go around.

THE SAVIOUR SAVES

In a high school, students were asked a hypothetical question in computer class. "Jesus

And Satan was doing a PowerPoint test. Just as they finished, a blackout came on, cutting off electricity. When electricity returns, who do you think wins?"

Jane answered, "Neither of them because they would have lost their data."

Julian replied, "Jesus wins because Jesus saves."

Moral: Faith in Jesus can bring light and success to your life.

MODERN MIRACLE

At school, students were asked to describe how Jesus healed the lame man. One student, whose parents always bought him the latest high-tech gadgets, wrote the following;

When a relative saw the lame man groaning on the floor, he quickly googled to find out where Jesus was. He called Jesus on his cell phone and politely requested Jesus' help. Inside five minutes, an impressive car pulled up at the lame man's residence. Jesus hurriedly came out of His limousine and rushed to the spot where the sick man lay. Miraculously, he picked him up, put him in the back seat, and sped off to the hospital, where the sick man was treated and finally healed.

The relative later texted Jesus a sincere note of thanks. Jesus tweeted, "No problem."

Moral: Technology can be a great tool if put to good use. But don't worship it as God.

GROTESQUE GOSSIP

Every year, an established Christian church holds a retreat for its priests to unwind, regroup, and strategize. Three priests teamed up in solitude after a long session. One of them suggested that they bare their chests to release stress. He said, "We all have moral failings. It will be good to confess. I will start. I am currently sweethearting two beautiful women at my church". To which the second added,' I have a weakness for gambling. I usually take money from the collection plate and sneak out to a gambling shop to play.' The third man of God was very shy and was reluctant to make his confession. Encouraged by the other two priests, he sheepishly said, 'I am a terrible gossip. "

Moral: Keep your skeleton secured in the closet. Free speech creates more stress than silence.

SACRED SINNERS

During a Sunday sermon at Christ the King Church, the pastor told the congregation that next week he would preach on the topic "Thou shalt not tell lies." He suggested that they read Matthew chapter 29.

Before he started the sermon the following week, he asked, 'How many of you read Matthew chapter 29? "All hands went up.

Pastor, "Matthew only has 28 chapters. Anyway, now to the sins of telling lies "

Moral: Lies can never be a cool, convenient Saviour. Truth sets you free and sinless.

SACRED STROKES

A local painter was contracted to paint a certain church before its grand opening. Whilst painting very slowly, he was singing 'Gentleee Jeessuus meeek aannd miilld plleeasse looook uppoon yoour littllee cchiildd'. The priest in charge heard him and noticed how tardy he was. So the good priest suggested that he paint faster so that the job could be finished before the opening.

Obediently, the guy painted faster and began to sing, "Paint you ass, paint you butt: paint you ass till it hurt ". Hearing that, the priest said, "Go back to your old tune before you defile this church."

Moral: The smarter the boss, the wiser the worker.

THE BEAUTY OF BLESSED BOOZE

A pastor in a certain church was preaching about the danger of drinking alcohol. He tried to demonstrate this contention by filling two glasses, one with pure gin and the other with pure water. He then placed a live worm in each glass and asked the congregation to observe very carefully. After some time, the worm in the gin wriggled to death while the one in the water was swimming happily.

Then the dutiful pastor asked, "In Jesus name, what lesson can you learn from that? "

An old woman in the back section of the church said in a loud voice, "When you get worms, drink gin."

Moral: Different perspectives or philosophies of life add spice to life to give it a lift.

A RIGHTEOUS REQUEST

A spiritually steadfast youth, prompted by wishful thinking, wrote a personal letter to Jesus asking for help. The letter was addressed to Jesus Christ

The Most High Lord

At the right hand of God

In Heaven above.

Workers at the local post office saw the letter and were curious about its contents.

They opened and read it. The boy had asked Jesus for 100 dollars. Knowing that such a letter would not reach that address to fulfill such a request. And out of good hearts

They raised $75 and sent it to the boy via return mail.

After he found the money in the envelope, he quickly wrote Jesus a thank-you note.

'Thank you, dear Jesus, for the cash. Next time you send me money, send it through.

Western Union and not by mail. The workers at the post office are dishonest and corrupt.

They opened the letter and stole $25 from the $100 I asked for."

Moral: Sometimes, when you do good, you end up holding the wood.

THE PUERILE PLEA

A very smart, gifted lad had a conversation with Jesus.

Lad, "Dear Jesus, you are so awesome and powerful that a million years is like a minute to you. "

Jesus, "That's right, son." "

Lad, 'Precious Lord, you are so great that a million dollars is like a cent to you."

Jesus: "You are right again, my child."

Lad, 'My benevolent and merciful Master, why don't you give me a million dollars? "

Jesus, "Sure, son, that's a piece of cake. Just hold on for a minute (million yrs)

Moral: No one can outwit the Lord in a lifetime, so don't mess with Him

WORSHIPPING WEALTH

A certain gentleman grew up to be a faithful Christian who regularly attended church.

Then, suddenly, he stopped going to church. One day, his former priest met him and asked him why he was not coming to church.

He said, "Father, to be brutally frank, I found a new Jesus, which is Money…wealth to worship…and I am so happy now. "

After several years, he returned to church, dejected and depressed. As soon as the priest saw him, he welcomed him with open arms like the prodigal son. He asked

"What brought you back to church? "

"Father, I am dead broke 'he coyly responded.

Moral: Money and material wealth are transient and fleeting, but God, your Savior, is

Everlasting. Be steadfastly holy in the name of the Lord.

THE DIVINE DUEL

There was a time when Jesus, Moses, and a Third Person were playing golf. Moses took

The first shot hit the ball within the green patch. "Good shot, Moses," Jesus said.

When Jesus struck the ball, it went and landed on a dry spot in the middle of a pond.

Jesus walked on the water and made a second swipe, which took the ball inches away from the hole. Moses complimented Jesus, "That was an excellent shot, my Lord."

When the Third Person hit the ball, it dropped in the pond, and a huge fish caught it in its mouth and spat it out to land near the hole. Then a squirrel appeared from nowhere and nudged it into the winning hole. And Jesus said, "Great shot, Dad. "

Moral: Whatever you do, don't mess with God because you will never win, no matter

How mighty you are.

RIVER OF RUM

In a rural Christian church, the pastor was preaching against the harm of drinking

alcohol. "If I had all the beer in the world, I would throw it in the river. If I had all the whiskey, wine, and rum of the world, I would dump them in the river."

He kept preaching about the problems caused by the use of alcohol. At the end of the sermon, the congregation in one high, hallowed alto sang the hymn, "Let's gather by the river. "

Moral: In teaching moderation, Jesus said, "Eat, drink, and be merry."

THE IMMACULATE CONCEPTION

A lady took her daughter to visit the doctor. "Doc, my 17-year-old daughter here is not feeling well. She complains of abdominal pains."

The good doctor took the girl into a private room for tests and examinations. After a while, he came out and told the lady that her daughter was four months pregnant.

"What! That's impossible. She hasn't met any man. She is a virgin being at home all the time.' She turned to her daughter and asked her if she had intercourse with anyone. "No, mama, "replied the girl. The doctor briskly walked across the room to a window and stared intently outside for the longest while. Impatient, the lady interrupted, "What happened, doc? Is something wrong outside?"

The doctor took a deep breath and slowly said, "I was looking for the bright Star and the three wise men from the east. I don't want to miss such an episode that happened a long time ago."

Moral: The immaculate Conception remains in the Bible; it does not happen in modern miracles.

THE VIRTOUS VIRGIN

A very devout woman has been a virgin all her life. She never got married nor had any relationship with any man. She vowed to remain a virgin. As a career woman, she got rich as she advanced in age. Anticipating death, she contracted an undertaker to etch selected words on her headstone:

'HEREIN LIES A VIRGIN WHO GAVE HER LIFE TO JESUS CHRIST'

When she died, the undertaker asked his gravediggers to etch those words on her headstone. The lazy grave workers thought it was too much work to put all those Words on, so they engraved the words' RETURNED UNOPENED.'

Moral: Be careful what you wish for. Jesus never asked for a sacrifice of such magnitude.

CRADLE OF CREATION

One day, a little girl in a Christian family asked her mom.

'Mom, where do humans come from?"

The mother thought for a while, then said, "God created Adam and Eve, who produced children who later produced more children, generation after generation. This process went on for centuries to create a world of people."

Later that day, she asked her dad in the garage the same question. Dad scratched his head and said, "A long time ago, there were apes and gorillas in Africa who evolved gradually to become human beings."

She then confronted her mom, "Mom, you said God created the human family. And Dad said people came from apes and gorillas."

"Your dad's family came from apes and gorillas," said Mom seriously.

Moral: The debate between Evolution and Creation has no end in the human family.

BLESSED BLASPHEME

A religious knowledge teacher asked her students. "Where can you find Jesus? "

One girl said, "In your heart ". Teacher approved.

Another girl said, "Jesus is found in all churches where Christian's worship."

The teacher supported and praised all positive answers.

Little Johnny said, "Jesus is found in the bathroom." The teacher, along with other students, was aghast. Then little Johnny explained, "This morning when my dad went to the bathroom and tried the door handle, he blurted out, 'Jesus Christ, you are still in there! "

Moral: Try to avoid blasphemous expressions by not sleeping in the bathroom.

WATER TO WINE

An Anglican priest who was speeding along the highway was overtaken and stopped by a

Cop. Seeing the white collar on his neck, the cop politely said, "Good morning, Father, please pull over."

Quickly and obediently, the pastor pulled over. "Father, you were speeding. You exceeded the speed limit for this road. "

He looked in the car and saw a half-full bottle of wine near the priest. "God forbid.

Are you drinking? "

The priest touched the bottle and said reverently, "Jesus, you did it again."

Moral: Don't blame Jesus for your moral indiscretions.

HEAVENLY HOIST

A religious teacher asked her class, "What must people do to go to heaven?"

One girl said, "You must clean the church and its surroundings." The Teacher agreed.

Another girl said, "You must be kind to elders. Help them cross the road; carry their grocery bags and run errands for them." The teacher said, "Great. "

One boy said, "You must be a good Christian. Go to church regularly to worship God and praise Jesus, your Saviour."

"Excellent," said the teacher.

Smart Alec said, "Miss, to go to heaven you must first have to die."

Moral: Just be a good, upright person and leave heaven for the hereafter.

SIN

Sin is the reason for Jesus' coming
Coming on a mission of saving and healing
'I come not to deal with the healthy and righteous
I came to call on the sinners and the unrighteous

When God surveyed the situation of Earthlings
He saw them swimming and drowning in sins
Showing mercy over this moral mess
He invoked the Incarnation to bring relief and redress

Divinely empowered Jesus arrived on the scene
As God in the blood and flesh of a human being
To confront the sins and evil of Satan
And to bring about the needed salvation

Jesus addressed all forms of sin.
Living through the thick and thin
Getting folks to confess and repent
Seeking forgiveness and spiritual strength

Knowing that iniquity and sickness stem from sins
He instructed people to change from within
Having faith and belief in God's goodness
Living a new life fashioned in forgiveness

Simply put, sin is a wrongdoing.
A moral defect and disease in a human being
An evil act sprang from a bad influence
Having serious, harmful consequences

Sin is a transgression against God's laws.
Disobedience and rebellion against divine cause
Devilish defiance against the Ten Commandments
Revealing crooked characters and evil achievements

Sin is the slick satan in us
Corrupting our conscience to depart from Jesus
And becoming victims of his temptation
On the horrible path to self-destruction

The cardinal sins in Christianity
Include pride, greed, and envy
Lust, wrath, sloth, and gluttony
And a wide host of companies

Other sins branch off from these categories
Murder, lies, blasphemy, cheating, and adultery
Cardinal sins are the root vices
With a multitude of their invoices

Greed gives birth to bribery and corruption
Stealing, exploitation, and discrimination
Based on the hunger for wealth, power, and fame
By players in the socio-economic and political game

Pride produces acts of arrogance.
Hypocrisy, haughtiness, vanity, and insolence
Practiced by folks who disregard humility
Having no respect for human dignity

Sloth is the unethical urge to ugliness
Of mind and body languishing in laziness
Not inclined to go out and work
Just waiting for freebies, handouts, and perks

Woe unto weaklings who wriggle in wrath
Ventilating the violence that fury has brought
Anger activates acute havoc and destruction
In those who can't control this evil emotion

Envy is engineered by competitive comparison.
Leads one to covet other people's possessions
A paralyzing psychological sin of the soul
Propelling people into the callous cold

Gluttony generates a greedy gumption for goodies
Selfishly grabbing everything, nothing for buddies
A sin of the stomach that stifles charity
Resulting in ill-health and obesity

Lust is a moral mistake of the flesh
Happened when the entire body is put to the test
Craving, longing, and yearning for carnal pleasure
From prospective clients or objects of desire

Jesus saw sins as trials and tribulations
As alluring, seductive schemes of Satan
Confronted by confession and repentance
Gaining forgiveness and spiritual deliverance

To Jesus, forgiveness is central to overcoming sins
Fast to forgive and free to be forgiven
Forgive your enemies and wrongdoers
And reconciliation will be blessed by our Father

The Creed

We believe in one God.
The Father, the Almighty
Maker of heaven and earth
Of all that is seen and unseen
We believe in one Lord, Jesus Christ
The only Son of God
Eternally begotten of the Father
God from Gog, Light from Light
True God from true God
Begotten, not made
Of being with the Father
Through Him all things were made
For us men and our salvation
He came down from heaven
By the power of the Holy Spirit
He became incarnate from the Virgin Mary
And was made man
For our sake, He was crucified under Pontius Pilate
He suffered death and was buried
On the third day, He rose again
In accordance with the Scriptures
He ascended into heaven
And is seated at the right hand of the Father
He will come again in glory
To judge the living and the dead
And His kingdom will have no end

We believe in the Holy Spirit
The Lord, the giver of life
Who proceed from the Father and the Son
With the Father and the Son
He is worshipped and glorified
He has spoken through the Prophets
We believe in one Holy catholic and Apostolic Church
We acknowledge one baptism for the forgiveness of sins
We look forward to the resurrection of the dead
And the life of the world to come. Amen